The FOOD JOURNAL of

Lewis & Clark

Recipes *for an* Expedition

Mary
Gunderson

Yankton, South Dakota

The Food Journal of Lewis & Clark: Recipes for an Expedition

Published by
History Cooks®
Post Office Box 709
Yankton, South Dakota 57078-0709 U.S.A.

Cover and text design © TLC Graphics, www.TLCGraphics.com
Cover and interior illustrations and maps by Dennis Dahlin
Back cover photo © M. Jensen Photography; Food styling by Lisa Golden Schroeder
Indian corn and feather photographs © gettyimages.com

First Printing 2003
Printed in the United States of America
10 9 8 7 6 5 4 3

The Library of Congress pre-assigned control number: 2002096191

Gunderson, Mary
    The food journal of Lewis & Clark: recipes for an expedition / Mary Gunderson.
    Yankton, SD: History Cooks, ©2003.
        176p. ;   cm.
    Includes bibliography, illustrations, maps, special recipe and contents indices.
    ISBN 0-9720391-0-4

    Presented in a chronological style, this book interweaves history and description of the historic Lewis and Clark expedition with discussions of their cooking methods. Includes recipes using food stuffs common in the 19th century, wild foods found along their journey, and some Native American foods.

    1. Lewis and Clark Expedition (1804-1806). 2. Cookery, American — Western style - History. 3. Food habits - West (U.S.) - History - 19th century. 4. Frontier and pioneer life - West (U.S.). 5. Clark, William, 1770-1838. 6. Lewis, Meriwether, 1774-1809. 7. West (U.S.) — Description and travel — to 1848. I. Title.

DDC 641.5978/09034 #b 21

Dedication

To Marian Boekelheide Gunderson

and to the memory of

Dexter H. Gunderson.

Other books by
Mary Gunderson

Today's Herbal Kitchen,
with the Memphis Herb Society

Cooking on the Lewis and Clark Expedition

Pioneer Farm Cooking

Cowboy Cooking

Oregon Trail Cooking

Southern Plantation Cooking

American Indian Cooking before 1500

Acknowledgments

THE AUTHOR APPRECIATES the generosity and expertise of the people who helped turn an idea into this book.

Thanks to Betty Fussell, James Ronda, and Mary Dodds Schlick for reviewing the manuscript. Thanks to the Lewis and Clark Trail Heritage Foundation (LCTHF), whose members demand rigorous standards of historical accuracy. A special thank you to past LCTHF board member Bev Hinds for reviewing my research at several stages. Thanks to past and present LCTHF board members Jim Peterson and Ron Laycock.

Thanks to the staffs of the American Philosophical Society, I.D. Weeks Library of the University of South Dakota, Library Company of Philadelphia, Library of Congress, Missouri Historical Society, Thomas Jefferson Historical Foundation, National Archives, National Capital Planning Commission, Schlesinger Library at Harvard University, South Dakota State Library, University of Nebraska Press, and Yankton Community Library.

For help with all manner of making the book, very special thanks for stellar work to Tamara Dever and Erin Stark of TLC Graphics, illustrator Dennis Dahlin, and editor Susan Derecskey. Thanks to Carolyn Acheson, Sandra Granseth, Gretchen Kauffman, and Krista Fritz Rogers for thoughtful comments and thorough results.

Thanks to John Anderson, Kris Anderson, Fred Baker, Pat Bell, Dale Bellisfield, Marlys Bielinski, Mary Pat Bierle, Joyce Brunken, Suzanne Brust and John Shepard, LouAnn and Tony Buquor, Bill Bushong, Elizabeth Chew, Holly Clegg, Suzanne Corbette, Colleen Craig-Davis, Susan Dosier, John Edge, Lisa Ekus, Glenda Embry, Allison Engel, Jim Fazio, Maureen Fischer, Val Frahm, Rod Gasch, Roscanne Gold, Billie Henderson, Kathryn Hagen and Tom Anderson, Bob Hansen, Judy Hauger, Hobby Hevewah, David Hinkley, Louise Holding Eagle, Jim Holmberg, Marilyn Hudson, Sarah Hutcheon, Kat Imhoff, Mike Jensen, Lydia King, Robin Kline, Joanne Kuster, Kathy Landis, Jim Luby, Karen Madson, Elaine Maruhn, Gary Moulton, Dan Moerman, Dorothy Molstad, Kathy Newton, Martha Nichols, Lyn Nielson, Diane Norton, Dave Ode, Sheila Oien, Bonnie Peterson, Ralph Pribble, Josiane and Bob Reinhardt, Karla Rupiper, Bob Rust, Delores Sand, Sharon Saunders, Fred Schneider, Jane Schneider, Jim Scholtz, Lisa Golden Schroeder, Sue Spalding and Mel Baughman, Sabrina Stavish, Gale Steves, Karen Van Lier, LeEtte and Lucas Vos, Kim Walter, Sue Weidner, Malinda Wiehle, Linda Wuebben, Diane Yanney, and David Zahrt. Thanks to Business Computing Services, Eisenbraun Engineering's office services, the Midwest Independent Publishers Association, and the Yankton taste panel crew.

Finally, many thanks to my mom and to my brother and his family—John Gunderson, Ann Schiefen, Andrew, and Annicka.

Table of Contents

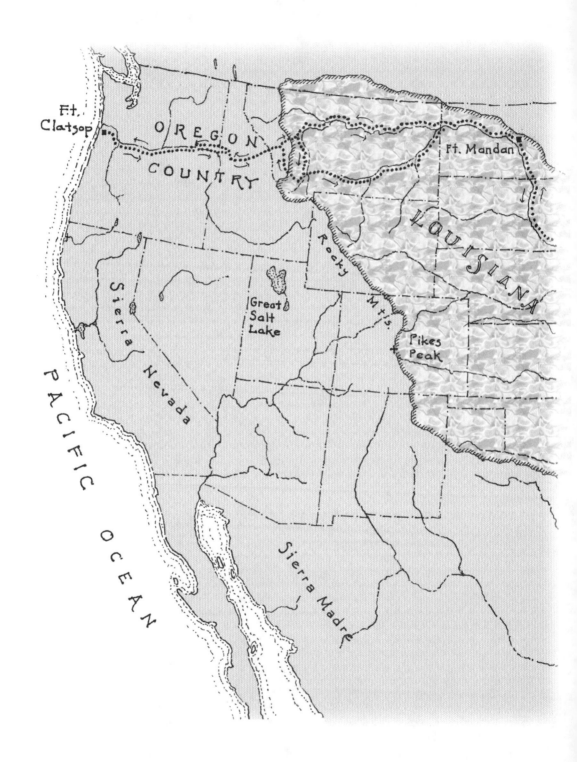

Ft.
Clatsop

OREGON

COUNTRY

Ft. Mandan

LOUISIANA

Rocky

Mts.

Pikes
Peak

Sierra
Nevada

Great
Salt
Lake

PACIFIC OCEAN

Sierra Madre

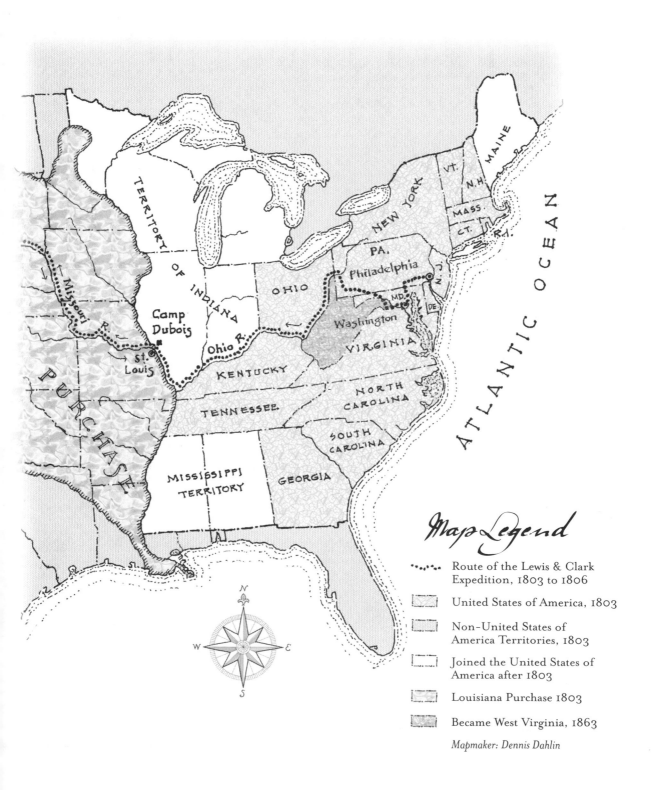

TERRITORY OF INDIANA

TERRITORY OF INDIANA

Camp Dubois

OHIO

Ohio R.

St. Louis

Missouri R.

PURCHASE

KENTUCKY

TENNESSEE

MISSISSIPPI TERRITORY

GEORGIA

NORTH CAROLINA

SOUTH CAROLINA

VIRGINIA

Washington

PA.

Philadelphia

MD.

DE

N.J.

NEW YORK

VT.

N.H.

MASS.

C.T.

R.I.

MAINE

ATLANTIC OCEAN

N
W   E
S

Map Legend

•••••• Route of the Lewis & Clark Expedition, 1803 to 1806

United States of America, 1803

Non-United States of America Territories, 1803

Joined the United States of America after 1803

Louisiana Purchase 1803

Became West Virginia, 1863

Mapmaker: Dennis Dahlin

INTRODUCTION

Recipes for an Expedition

MUCH OF MY life, I have lived near a portion of the Lewis and Clark Trail in what is now South Dakota. My great-grandparents settled along the Missouri River sixty years after the Expedition passed this way. Several of the Expedition landmarks are among my geographic touchstones, including Spirit Mound, near present-day Vermillion, South Dakota, and Calumet Bluff, near Yankton, South Dakota. I am one of thousands of people for whom the Lewis and Clark Expedition is as much personal history as American history.

When I first considered writing about foods of the Lewis and Clark Expedition seven years ago, I wondered if the food tasted good. From my work as a food writer and culinary historian, I had to determine if it made sense to recreate Expedition foods for modern people and sensibilities. While reading the Lewis and Clark journals and letters, I discovered that Meriwether Lewis and William Clark wrote about food almost every day. The more startling entries—eating several pounds of meat or dining on tainted meat—are offset by the countless other details of gustatory satisfaction.

A picture of daily life across early nineteenth-century North America begins to emerge, starting with the culinary pursuits of the Expedition's originator, Thomas Jefferson, with the dynamic culinary climate in Philadelphia where Lewis made journey preparations, and through the food wisdom and practices of the people in each American Indian tribe who made contact with the Expedition.

We know when the explorers ate the last of their butter and when they first tasted buffalo. Lewis delighted in Toussaint Charbonneau's *boudin blanc*. John Ordway, one of the sergeants, praised the Mandan and Hidatsa women who prepared corn, beans, and squash for the visitors during the winter of 1804 to 1805. Both Lewis and Ordway recorded the day, 4 July 1805, when the Corps of Discovery drank their last whiskey rations. After the harrowing seventeen days spent crossing the Bitterroot Mountains, the command, near starvation, gratefully received hospitality from the Nez Percé who offered food from their abundant stores of roots, berries, nuts, and fish. Sacagawea saved wheat flour and made a kind of biscuit for her son, Jean Baptiste, and shared some with William Clark during the winter at Fort Clatsop.

In seeking to understand the Lewis and Clark Expedition in terms of food, I have traveled across time and cultures. I have combed the journals the travelers kept and relied on a wide range of research about the Expedition and its members, as well as information about everyday lives across the continent in the early 1800s. My key written sources have been the words of Meriwether Lewis, William Clark, Thomas Jefferson, and others, especially as found in *The Journals of the Lewis and Clark Expedition*, volumes 1 to 13, as edited by Gary Moulton, and *The Letters of the Lewis and Clark Expedition*, as edited by Donald Jackson. James Ronda's *Lewis and Clark Among the Indians*, Paul Cutright's *Lewis and Clark: Pioneering Naturalists*, and Daniel E. Moerman's *Native American Ethnobotany* each gave me insight and perspective. Besides dozens of other written sources, including cookbooks and recipes from the early 1800s, I've talked with experts about such subjects as sausage making, grape varieties, basketry, corn parching, Latin names for plants and animals, and much more.

I have applied these facts and inquiries to what I call paleocuisineology®—bringing history alive through cooking—to make a history book with recipes.

Welcome to the table of the Lewis and Clark Expedition. The dining cloth reaches across the North American continent, circa 1803 to 1806. There is more than enough room for each of us to crowd around. Linger at any point in the journey and a rich food history is at hand, revealing the larger story of the Expedition and its still-felt impact on our national consciousness. Such is the power of food. Dig in!

23 February
1801

Jefferson to Lewis[i]

"[The job] would make you know & be known to characters of influence in the affairs of our country, and give you the advantage of their wisdom. You would of course save also the expence of subsistence & lodging as you would be one of my family."

10 March 1801

Lewis to Jefferson[ii]

"... to express a wish that I should accept the place of your private Secretary; I most cordially acquiesce, and with pleasure accept the office, nor were further motives necessary to induce my compliance, than that you Sir should conceive that in the discharge of the duties of that office, I could be servicable to my country or ucefull to yourself...."

4

CHAPTER ONE

*Washington, D.C.
1801 to 1803*

Jefferson's Vision

MERIWETHER LEWIS JOINED President Thomas Jefferson as his private secretary in early 1801. Lewis served the president while Jefferson conducted affairs of state. During Lewis's tenure, both men focused on the president's vision to launch an exploration of the western lands of the continent.

Lewis dined often with Jefferson, who took great care to eat excellent food and drink pleasing spirits (see page 14). Later, Lewis at times compared Expedition fare to his memories of fine cuisine (see pages 94 and 121).

No record exists that Lewis visited Monticello while he served the president. But Jefferson had food supplies brought regularly from his Virginia plantation in addition to produce from the garden he had established in Washington.

Jefferson's Enthusiasms: At Table and in the Garden

No other United States president comes close to Jefferson in his keen study of the garden, the foods he ate, and the spirits he drank. Jefferson collected and recorded recipes in French and English, including those for pasta, meringues, ice cream, and yellow plum tomato preserves. He loved salads and even planted sesame seeds to be processed into oil for dressings. Jefferson once wrote that he preferred vegetables as the bulk of his diet. He faithfully kept his "Garden Kalendar" from 1809 until his death in 1826.

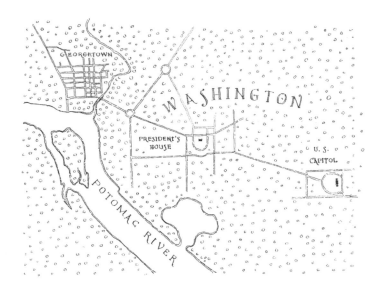

Jefferson took a particular interest in the seeds and cuttings that Lewis and Clark had gathered during the Expedition. In 1807, Jefferson wrote that he planted Arikara beans, corn from the Arikara or the Mandan, and Missouri salsify.

Later Known as the White House

During Jefferson's presidency, the chief executive's residence bore the official name the President's House. In the 1850s, the name was changed to Executive Mansion. Informally, the building was called the White House from 1798 when its walls received their first coat of lime wash. Theodore Roosevelt changed the official name to the White House in 1902.

A Job Offer from the President

The twenty-seven-year-old Lewis had seven years experience in the U.S. Army when he was asked to join the president's staff. He had achieved the rank of captain at the age of twenty-six and had served on the frontier in what is now Ohio. The Lewis family and Thomas Jefferson were neighbors and friends in Virginia. Lewis's five years of school passed for a significant formal education at the time.

Lewis at Table

There is at least one reference to Lewis's presence with Jefferson for official affairs. The Reverend Manasseh Cutler, a Massachusetts congressman, co-author of the Northwest Ordinance (1787), and fellow of the American Philosophical Society, left a record of an evening with Jefferson, Lewis, and perhaps others. Reverend Cutler commented to Lewis that the savory pie seemed to be **"filled with strillions of onions, or shallots....tasted very strong, and not agreeable."**[iii] Lewis advised Cutler that the dish was Italian in origin and was made with flour, butter, and strong spirits, though Jefferson's written recipe does not include liquor.

WASHINGTON, D.C.
1801 TO 1803

Virginia-Style Beaten Biscuits

THE TENDER FOLDS of these biscuits have long been a preferred vehicle for slices of country ham. Do not expect the fluffiness of a baking powder biscuit. Few families enjoyed these biscuits if they did not have servants to spend twenty to thirty minutes beating air into the dough.

I cup bread flour

I cup whole wheat flour

I/2 teaspoon salt

I/4 cup butter

I/2 cup water, milk, or half-and-half, plus I tablespoon, if necessary

Country ham (see Mail-Order Sources, page 155), for serving

Process the flour and salt with the butter in food processor 2 or 3 times. Add the water and process for 2 minutes.

Remove the dough from the processor bowl. On a lightly floured board, fold the dough over itself several times. Roll 1/4 inch thick. Prick with a fork every 2 inches. Cut with a floured biscuit cutter. Place the biscuits on a greased baking sheet. Bake at 325°F for about 30 minutes. Serve immediately. (The biscuits are best served immediately. They toughen when cooled.)

Good to eat with thin slices of country ham tucked in the place where the biscuit opens.

Makes 8 to 12 biscuits.

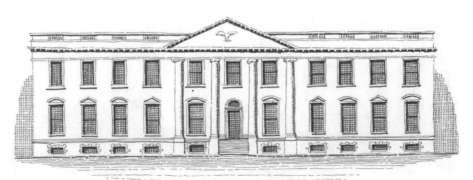

Brandied Spiced Peaches

JEFFERSON'S HANDWRITTEN RECIPE for Brandied Spiced Peaches was recorded in French. Both sugar and brandy are lightened in this version.

2 pounds fresh peaches

I cup sugar

1/2 teaspoon whole cloves

4 to 6 tablespoons brandy

Ice cream, pound cake, or angel food cake, for serving

Carefully add whole peaches, one or two at a time, to a large saucepan three-quarters full of boiling water. After 30 seconds, remove the peaches with a slotted spoon. Cool slightly. Peel and slice the peaches. Repeat with the remaining peaches. Set aside and drain the water.

In the same saucepan, bring the sugar, 3/4 cup of water, and the cloves to a boil over medium-high heat. Boil for 7 to 10 minutes. Add the peach slices and brandy. Return to a boil and cook for 2 to 4 minutes, or until the peaches are tender.

Remove the pan from the heat and evenly spoon the fruit into 2 one-pint jars with tight lids. Carefully divide and pour the syrup over the fruit. Cool before covering tightly. Store in the refrigerator for up to 3 months.

To serve, spoon over ice cream, pound cake, or angel food cake.

Makes 2 pints.

Harvest Mincemeat

BEFORE ELECTRICITY AND the later inventions of the refrigerator and freezer, food preservation often depended on adding sugar, salt, or alcohol. The idea for mincemeat traveled easily from its origins in the British Isles to the kitchens and dining rooms of the young United States. Mincemeat showed up on holiday tables after the fall harvest (raisins and apples) and butchering (the beef). Many traditional mincemeat recipes call for added suet. This version is rich enough without it.

1 pound lean ground beef (85% lean)

2 cups chopped, peeled apples, such as Braeburn, which hold their shape during cooking

2 cups raisins

3/4 cup (firmly packed) brown sugar

1 cup apple cider

1 cup brandy

1/2 teaspoon ground cinnamon

1/2 teaspoon ground cloves

1/2 teaspoon ground nutmeg

Pastry or ice cream, for serving

Cook the ground beef until lightly browned, 5 to 7 minutes. Stir in the apples, raisins, brown sugar, cider, brandy, and spices. Cook, uncovered, over medium-low heat for about 2 1/2 hours, or until the mixture thickens and caramelizes, stirring occasionally. Or place in an ovenproof dish and bake, uncovered, at 300°F for about 2 1/2 hours.

Cool. Serve over pastry or ice cream. Refrigerate for up to 1 month or freeze for up to 3 months.

Makes about 6 cups mincemeat or forty-eight 2-tablespoon servings.

Fresh Peas with Mint-Butter Sauce

JEFFERSON, THE PRIVILEGED, well-traveled, and multilingual American aristocrat, believed that a nation of farmers—educated farmers—would be the strongest foundation for the United States. Jefferson did his part as he directed and observed his own gardens at Monticello and at his Washington home. He once wrote that English peas were his favorite vegetable.

4 cups fresh or frozen peas (about 4 pounds in pod)

1/3 cup chopped green onions (about 5 onions with greens)

1 tablespoon butter

1 teaspoon chopped fresh mint

1/4 teaspoon salt

Place the peas in cold water just to cover (1/4 cup water for frozen; 1 cup water for fresh). Bring to a boil, uncovered, over medium-high heat. Cook 10 minutes for freshly shelled peas, 3 to 5 minutes for frozen peas. During the last minute of cooking, stir in the chopped green onions. Drain the peas and place in a serving dish. Toss with the butter, mint leaves, and salt. Serve immediately.

Makes 6 to 8 servings.

WASHINGTON, D.C.
1801 TO 1803

Monticello Muffins

A VERSION OF this labor-intensive recipe exists in Jefferson's hand. Also known as English muffins, these muffins have an uneven honeycomb texture best retained by splitting with the tines of a fork instead of with a knife.

2 1/2 cups bread flour

4 teaspoons active dry yeast

2 teaspoons salt

1 teaspoon sugar

1 1/2 cups warm milk or water (120°F)

2 tablespoons melted butter or oil

1 cup whole wheat flour

Brown rice flour

Combine 1 1/2 cups of the bread flour, the yeast, salt, and sugar in a mixer bowl. Stir in the milk and butter and beat at low speed for about 1 minute. Beat at medium speed for 2 minutes.

Add the remaining bread flour and the whole wheat flour to make a dough. Beat well for 3 to 5 minutes. If too stiff for the mixer, beat by hand with a wooden spoon, 5 to 7 minutes. Mix until smooth. The mixture will be too sticky to knead. Place in an oiled bowl and let rise until doubled, about 50 minutes.

Dust a greased baking sheet with brown rice flour. Shape the dough into 12 rounds, about 4 inches across and 3/4 inch thick. Cover with a clean dishtowel and let rise for 35 to 40 minutes, or until doubled in height. Muffins will lose their shape if they rise too long.

Bake the muffins in a heavy skillet or on a griddle over medium heat, 8 to 10 minutes on each side. Turn more than once if muffins appear to brown too fast.

Makes about 12 muffins.

Raised Waffles

WAFFLES BAKED ON a hot, flat surface evolved from wafers used for the Communion sacrament in Christian churches. By the nineteenth century, a larger waffle iron had been invented and waffles were on the menu in Jefferson's home and in many others. Yeast gives the waffles a fluffier texture and fuller flavor than those made with baking powder.

2 cups whole wheat flour

1 cup all-purpose flour

1 tablespoon active dry yeast

1 tablespoon (firmly packed) brown sugar

1 teaspoon salt

1/4 cup melted butter

2 cups warm milk or water (120°F)

2 eggs

Combine 1 cup of the whole wheat flour and 1/2 cup of the all-purpose flour, the yeast, brown sugar, salt, and butter in a mixer bowl. Stir in the warm milk and beat on low speed for 1 minute. Beat on medium speed for 1 minute more. Add the remaining flour and beat until smooth, 1 to 2 minutes. Let stand at 75° to 80°F, covered with a clean cloth, for 4 hours or overnight.

When ready to bake, beat the eggs into the mixture. Heat a waffle iron according to the manufacturer's directions. Pour 1/3 cup batter into each segment of the hot iron. Bake until golden brown; baking time will vary with the waffle maker. Serve immediately with honey or jam.

Makes about 14 waffles.

WASHINGTON, D.C.
1801 TO 1803

The Louisiana Purchase

THOMAS JEFFERSON ENVISIONED the United States of America stretching from the Atlantic to the Pacific as early as his service as envoy to France and his term as Secretary of State. Before engaging Meriwether Lewis, Jefferson had made one serious effort toward sending an exploratory mission across the continent.

During that time, control of the territory called Louisiana had volleyed between Spain and France. France claimed rights to the territory when the emperor Napoleon offered the territory to Jefferson. Napoleon needed the cash for his efforts to conquer and rule Europe. The leaders' representatives completed the Louisiana transaction in the spring of 1803: nine hundred thousand acres in exchange for fifteen million dollars.

The president, however, had already authorized Lewis to prepare for the Expedition and had secured both French and British passports for him. The outright sale of Louisiana to the Americans made Jefferson all the more determined to secure control of the north-western lands as well, where the British had a presence due in part to Alexander Mackenzie's 1789 and 1793 journeys across the Rocky Mountains in what is now Canada.

i. *Thomas Jefferson Papers*, Manuscript Division, Library of Congress.

ii. Ibid.

iii. Evan Jones, *American Food: The Gastronomic Story* (New York: E.P. Dutton, 1975), 33.

Notes

On his way to
Philadelphia,
Lewis stopped in
Harpers Ferry to
buy guns for the
Expedition.
He received this
special request
from the president,
who maintained
a reputation for
collecting and serving
fine cognac, wines,
sherry, Madeira,
Burgundies, and
Sauternes.

2o April 1803

Jefferson to Lewis[1]

*"Will you be so good as
to call on Doctr. Bollman
with my compliments &
pay him for some wine
sent me? I suppose it
will be about 12 Doll.
But it must be whatever
he says."*

14

CHAPTER TWO

*Philadelphia
May to June 1803*

Lewis Receives Instruction and Buys Provisions

PRESIDENT JEFFERSON ARRANGED for Meriwether Lewis to accomplish further journey preparations in Philadelphia. Lewis kept appointments with leading thinkers of the day—Robert Patterson, mathematics and navigation; Dr. Benjamin Rush, human medicine; Dr. Benjamin Smith Barton, botany; and Dr. Caspar Wistar, anatomy and fossils—all members of the American Philosophical Society, as was Jefferson.

From May to early June, Lewis met with these men to continue building his storehouse of scientific knowledge as directed by the president. Equally important, Lewis secured all manner of provisions. With the help of Philadelphia purveyor Israel Whelen, Lewis bought Portable Soup (see page 18), brass kettles, tin tumblers, and metal spoons, as well as beads, especially China blues (to trade for food with tribal communities), cloth, writing materials, and equipment for hunting and fishing.

The United States' Premier City

In 1803, Philadelphia rated as the largest city in the seventeen United States of America and was considered the best. The sixth and seventh largest cities were its then suburbs of

Southwark and Northern Liberties. Philadelphia had been the national capital for ten years, during the presidencies of George Washington and John Adams. Benjamin Franklin, one of America's most creative leaders, had made his home there. The city pulsed with invention, ideas, and commerce. Philadelphia radiated exuberance and intelligence. Between appointments and responsibilities, Lewis may have enjoyed the local turtle delicacy, terrapin, or met friends for a glass of Fish House punch.

His choices for food and spirits were the best in the United States. Philadelphia's merchants did business with England, France, and the Caribbean sugar plantations. Coffee arrived from both South America and Java. The British East India Company supplied tea from China. America's first ice cream store started in Philadelphia. Baking traditions from England and Germany thrived.

Lewis at Leisure in Philadelphia

Lewis's work and study in Philadelphia mingled with social visits with the city's luminaries. On both 15 May and 19 May 1803, the adjutant general of Pennsylvania, Mahlon Dickerson, recorded in his journal that he dined with Lewis. On 19 May, they were the guests of merchant Henry Sheaff, who had supplied wine to George and Martha Washington during their Philadelphia years.

PHILADELPHIA
MAY TO JUNE 1803

Philadelphia Provisions
[partial listing]

Camp equipage	WT. [POUNDS]	[$ COST]
32 tin cannisters of P[ortable] Soup	193	8
3 doz: Pint Tumblers	6 1/2	4.20
125 Large fishg Hooks		4.45
Fishg Lines assorted	10 1/2	18.09
1 Stand of Fishg [Lines] with hooks Complete	3	
1 Sportsmans flaske		1.50
6 Brass Kettles & Porterage 25 cts.	28	15.18
1 block tin Sauce pan	3/4	1.50
1 Corn Mill	20	9
1 Set of Gold Scales & Wts.	1/4	2.33
1 Rule	1 oz	60
1 Sett Iron Weights	4	75
2 pr. Large Shears	3 1/2	1.86
2 doz: Table Spoons	3	1.87
4 drawing Knives	2 1/2	1.20
1 1/4 doz. Small cord	8 1/2	1.79
2 Hatchets		83
1 Wetstone	4 1/2	47
2 p. Pocket steel yards		47
Pkg 12 lbs. Castile Soap	2	1.68

Philadelphia Provisions[ii], continued

Arms & Accoutrements & Ammn.	WT. [POUNDS]	[$ COST]
1 Pair Pocket pistols (P. by L.)		10
176 lb. Gun powder	176	155.75
52 leaden Cannisters for Gunpowr	420	26.33
15 Powder Horns & Pouches		26.25

FROM PUBLIC STORE

15 Powder Horns

18 Tomahaws

15 Scalpking Knives & Belts

15 Gun Slings

30 Brushes & Wires

15 Cartouch[e] Boxes

15 painted Knapsacks

500 Rifle Flints

125 Musket [Flints]

50 lb. best rifle Powder

1 pr. Horseman's Pistols

420 lbs. Sheet Lead

Provisions & c

	WT.	[$ COST]
193 lbs. P. Soup	193	289.50
30 Galls. Spr. of Wine in 6 Kegs		77.20
		366.70

TOTAL TRIP COST: 1803 dollars: $38,722.35

TOTAL TRIP COST: 2002 dollars: $614,640.48

Portable Soup

LONG SIMMERING TIMES coax proteins from the meat and bones. French chefs use the same method with added seasonings to make brown sauce or *demi-glace*, the flavor heart of many sauces. For a simple meat soup made with Portable Soup, see page 108.

This recipe makes 193 pounds of Portable Soup if you start with 772 pounds of oxtails.

5 to 6 pounds oxtails	2 carrots, peeled and cut in half
1 large onion, peeled and quartered	1 1/2 teaspoons salt
	1 bay leaf

Trim fat from the oxtails. Combine the meat, vegetables, salt, and bay leaf in a 5-quart kettle. Add enough water to cover the meat. Bring to a boil and reduce the heat to keep the broth just below the boil. Skim and discard the residue from the surface with a fine mesh strainer. Continue to skim the residue from the surface for the next 30 to 45 minutes.

Add 2 cups water, cover, and let the broth simmer gently for about 4 hours. Skim periodically when residue rises to the surface. The more you skim, the clearer the final product will be. Add about 4 cups more water. Cover and continue to simmer gently for 4 to 5 hours more.

When the meat has fallen off the bones, pour the stock through a cheesecloth-lined strainer into a large bowl. Discard the meat, bones, vegetables, and bay leaf. Cover the stock and refrigerate.

The stock will be a quivering, gelled mass. Skim the fat from the surface. Spoon the gel into a 3-quart kettle. Discard any residue remaining in the bottom of the bowl. Bring the gel to a rolling boil for about 45 minutes, or until the stock is syrupy, slightly thickened, and golden brown. Skim any residue. Place a wooden spoon in the kettle during the boil to prevent the stock from boiling over.

Portable Soup, continued

Pour the stock 1/2 to 3/4 inch deep in four 9-inch pie plates or 9-inch square baking dishes. Lightly cover and refrigerate.

Peel the Portable Soup from each pie plate. Cut into 3 1/2-inch squares and wrap individually. Place in a container with a tight seal. Keeps indefinitely. For best flavor, store in the refrigerator or freezer. For an authentic 1803 to 1806 flavor, store at room temperature indefinitely.

Makes about 1 1/2 pounds Portable Soup.

The Bouillon Cube's Ancestor

FROM THE 1750s, Portable Soup, also called Pocket Soup, was produced commercially, especially for such customers as Britain's Royal Navy Victualling Office and for the young United States military and its soldiers and sailors. Soldiers and travelers from Hungary to England recorded using some form of Portable Soup for hundreds of years before that.

The first person to make Portable Soup probably left meat bones simmering over an open fire, leaving the mixture to boil almost dry. The cook, being frugal, saved what was left. Over time, observant cooks probably noticed that the remains did not go rancid if the fat was skimmed. Just as we add water to concentrated cubes or packets of powdered soup, those travelers added water to Portable Soup to make either a savory broth by itself or, if there were vegetables and meat to add, a thick soup.

The purveyor Israel Whelen supplied one hundred ninety-three pounds of Portable Soup made by cook François Baillet packed in canvas oilcloth and sealed with wax. Lewis paid $289.50 ($4,595.24 in 2002 dollars). His forethought in packing the gluey soup concentrate paid off in the fall of 1805 when supplies were low and hunting was scarce (see page 108).

Chicken Fricassée

FRICASSÉE COMES FROM the French word *fricasser*, which means to cut up and stew a small animal or bird. Americans adopted the French word and cooking style, especially as it refers to Chicken Fricassée.

One 2- to 3-pound whole chicken, cut up

Boiling water

6 ribs celery, halved

I cup pearl onions, peeled (about I pound)

2 medium carrots, peeled and cut into 2 x I/2-inch pieces

I bay leaf

I cup milk

I/2 cup all-purpose flour

I/4 cup white wine

I teaspoon salt

I/2 teaspoon freshly ground black pepper

Place the chicken in a 3-quart kettle with a lid and cover with boiling water, about 8 cups. Add the celery, onions, carrots, and bay leaf. Simmer, uncovered, over medium-low heat for about 50 minutes. Chicken will be more tender if the mixture does not boil. Remove the chicken and vegetables to a platter and cover to keep warm. Skim fat, if necessary. Measure 3 cups broth. Reserve the remaining broth, if any, for other dishes.

Mix the milk and flour in a jar with a tight-fitting lid. Cover and shake well for about 30 seconds until well combined. Pour the milk-flour mixture into the broth and heat to a boil, stirring constantly. Boil for about 3 minutes, or until the mixture thickens. Stir in the wine, salt, and pepper, and cook for 4 minutes more.

Pour the sauce evenly over the chicken and vegetables on a serving platter. Serve immediately.

Makes 4 to 6 servings.

Pepperpot

"PEPPERPOT! ALL HOT!" Lewis may have stopped to buy a bowl of Pepperpot on his way home from conferring with a mentor or visiting the alehouse. African-"American" women sold bowls of Pepperpot from portable brazier-heated pots on street corners and in markets.

The dish can be traced to African and Spanish influences in the Caribbean islands. In Philadelphia, Pepperpot became a local favorite, limited only by a cook's ingredients and imagination. This version focuses on the unique texture of beef tripe, the lining from one or both of the animal's stomachs, plus potatoes and a tame amount of red pepper, black peppercorns, and freshly ground black pepper.

1/2 pound honeycomb or plain beef tripe or mild pork sausage

1 cup milk

3/4 pound cross-cut beef shank

1 teaspoon whole black peppercorns

2 to 3 medium potatoes, peeled and diced

1 large onion, peeled and chopped

1 small red hot pepper, seeded and finely chopped

1 to 1 1/2 teaspoons freshly ground black pepper

1 to 1 1/2 teaspoons salt

1 teaspoon dried marjoram

1/2 teaspoon dried thyme

Rinse the tripe under cool water. Drain. Soak the tripe in the milk in a medium bowl for about 20 minutes. Drain and discard milk. If using pork sausage, there is no need to rinse or soak. (Soaking freshens the taste of the tripe and improves the soup's flavor.)

Combine the tripe, beef shank, peppercorns, and about 8 cups water. Simmer, uncovered, over medium-low heat for about 1 hour. Do not allow to boil.

Strain the broth and reserve. Chop the tripe and trim the meat from the shank bone, discarding the fat and bone. If using sausage, skim fat from surface. Return tripe and meat to pan. Add enough water to the broth to make 6 1/2 cups. Stir in the potatoes, onion, chopped pepper, black pepper, salt, marjoram, and thyme.

Bring to a boil. Reduce the heat to medium. Simmer, uncovered, about 30 minutes, or until the potatoes are tender. Serve immediately.

Makes about 10 servings.

Scrapple

IN EARLY PHILADELPHIA, savory pork, buckwheat, and cornmeal puddings known as *pan haus* came to be called scrapple. Versions of scrapple traveled west across the continent through the nineteenth and early twentieth centuries. The gently seasoned pillar of ordinary foods has become an American classic. Feel free to substitute other cuts of pork or change the seasoning to suit your palate.

I pound pork shoulder

I large onion, peeled and sliced

10 whole peppercorns

I bay leaf

3/4 cup stone-ground cornmeal

1/2 cup buckwheat flour

I teaspoon salt

1/2 teaspoon ground nutmeg

I teaspoon fresh thyme, chopped, or 1/2 teaspoon dried thyme

Place the pork shoulder, 6 cups of water, the onion, peppercorns, and bay leaf in a 3-quart saucepan. Bring to a boil. Reduce the heat. Simmer for about I hour, or until the pork is tender. Remove the meat from the broth. Shred the meat with 2 forks. Discard the bones.

Strain the broth. Measure 4 cups of strained broth into a 3-quart saucepan. Stir in the shredded pork, cornmeal, buckwheat, salt, nutmeg, and thyme. Bring to a boil, stirring almost constantly. Reduce the heat to medium-low and continue cooking until the mixture thickens, 5 to 10 minutes, stirring frequently to prevent lumps.

Spoon into a well-greased 8 x 4-inch loaf pan. Cover and chill in the refrigerator for several hours or overnight.

To serve, cut into slices and fry in hot oil. Scrapple is traditionally served with fried eggs.

Makes 6 to 8 servings.

Apees Cookies

THE DELICATE BALANCE of rosewater with caraway seeds makes Apees Cookies something to savor. Also called A.P.s or Apeas, they are dunking cookies and considered a Philadelphia specialty. The cookies are distinct from Apeas Cakes, a Pennsylvania Dutch gingerbread. This version was inspired by Eliza Leslie, who studied cooking with Elizabeth Goodfellow and who later wrote her own cookbooks, including *Miss Leslie's Directions for Cookery*.[iii]

3/4 cup butter

1 cup powdered sugar
(about 1/2 pound)

1 egg

2 tablespoons rosewater
(see Note)

2 cups all-purpose flour

1 tablespoon caraway seeds

1/2 teaspoon ground cinnamon

1/2 teaspoon ground nutmeg

1/4 teaspoon salt

Flour and sugar for
rolling cookies

Beat together the butter and sugar. Beat in the egg and rosewater. By hand, stir in the flour, spices, and salt. Cover and chill in the refrigerator for about 20 minutes.

To form the cookies, mix equal portions of flour and sugar and sprinkle on the work surface. Roll the dough 1/4 inch thick. Cut with a 2 1/2-inch biscuit cutter. Transfer to ungreased baking sheets. Bake at 350°F for 12 to 15 minutes on the middle rack of the oven until the cookies are light golden brown. Store in an airtight container in the refrigerator or freezer.

Makes 36 cookies.

NOTE: Available by mail order or in specialty stores.

23

PHILADELPHIA
MAY TO JUNE 1803

Cinnamon Buns

PHILADELPHIA BAKERS DREW from English and German traditions to establish the city's reputation for bread baking. Businesses supplied Hardtack Biscuits (see page 70) to merchant ships and vendors sold hot Cinnamon Buns on the street.

DOUGH

3 to 3 1/2 cups bread flour

2 cups whole wheat flour

1/2 cup granulated sugar

4 1/2 teaspoons active dry yeast

1 teaspoon salt

3/4 cup warm milk (120°F)

1/2 cup warm water (120°F)

1/4 cup melted butter

2 eggs

FILLING

1 to 2 tablespoons melted butter

1/2 cup (firmly packed) brown sugar

1 tablespoon ground cinnamon

1/2 cup raisins

GLAZE

2 cups powdered sugar

2 to 4 tablespoon milk or water

2 teaspoons vanilla extract

To make the dough, combine 1 1/2 cups of the bread flour, 1 cup of the whole wheat flour, the sugar, yeast, and salt in a mixer bowl. Stir in the milk, water, and melted butter. Mix for 1 minute on low. Mix for 2 minutes on medium speed. Beat in the eggs. Stir in 1 1/2 cups of the bread flour and the remaining 1 cup whole wheat flour to form a soft dough. Add the remaining bread flour by the tablespoon if the dough is still too wet.

Turn the dough onto a floured surface. Knead the dough until smooth, about 5 minutes. Cover with a clean towel and let rise in warm place (75° to 80°F) until doubled, about 1 hour. Lightly grease two 9-inch round baking pans. Set aside.

To make the buns, place the dough on a lightly floured surface. Form into 2 balls. Roll the first ball into a 14 x 9-inch rectangle. Brush with about 1 tablespoon melted butter. Combine the brown sugar and cinnamon in a small bowl. Sprinkle the dough with half of the sugar mixture. Sprinkle with 1/4 cup

Cinnamon Buns, continued

of the raisins. Roll up from the long side. Cut into 12 pieces and place in a baking pan. Repeat with the second ball. Cover with a clean towel and let rise in a warm place (75° to 80°F) until doubled, 30 to 45 minutes. Bake in a preheated 375°F oven (350°F for a glass baking dish) for 20 to 25 minutes, or until the buns are golden brown and the center buns sound hollow when tapped. Let cool for 5 minutes.

To glaze the buns, turn the buns out onto wire racks. Make a glaze with the powdered sugar mixed with milk or water and vanilla and drizzle the buns with the glaze.

Makes 2 dozen buns.

CARAMEL BUNS: Reduce the cinnamon to 1 teaspoon and omit the raisins in the filling. After greasing the pans and preparing the buns, sprinkle each pan with 1/2 cup (firmly packed) brown sugar mixed with 1/4 cup melted butter; evenly arrange 1/3 cup whole pecans over the sugar mixture. Arrange the buns over the sugar-pecan mixture. Continue as above. After baking, omit the glaze.

25

Lemon Ice Cream

CITIZENS OF PHILADELPHIA had their choice of ice cream flavors and shapes from the late 1700s on. The brisk trade with the Caribbean made lemons widely available for recipe experimentation.

2 cups whipping cream
2 cups half-and-half
1/2 pound powdered sugar

Juice and grated zest of 2 lemons (about 1/4 cup juice and 2 teaspoons grated zest)

Beat all the ingredients in a large bowl. Pour into an ice cream freezer container, filling up to two-thirds full. Follow the manufacturer's directions, using 6 parts ice to 1 part rock salt.

Eat immediately (be sure to lick the paddle) or place the canister in the freezer for 2 to 4 hours to ripen the ice cream.

Makes 1 quart ice cream.

Raspberry Ice Cream

LEWIS AND CLARK picked and ate fresh and dried huckleberries (*Vaccinium v.*), buffalo berries (*Shepherdia argentea*), Juneberries, also known as serviceberries (*Amelanchier v.*), and many others. Perhaps Lewis ate them remembering fresh Raspberry Ice Cream enjoyed on a hot June day in Philadelphia.

4 cups fresh or
frozen raspberries

1/2 pound powdered sugar

2 cups whipping cream

2 cups half-and-half

Place the raspberries in a large bowl and toss with the sugar. Let stand about 1 hour. Press out the juice through a sieve to measure about 2 cups raspberry juice, free of seeds. If you like the crunch of seeds in the ice cream, omit this step.

Add the cream and half-and-half and beat well. Pour the mixture into an ice cream freezer container and fill up to two-thirds full. Follow the manufacturer's directions, using 6 parts ice to 1 part rock salt.

Eat immediately (be sure to lick the paddle) or place the canister in the freezer for 2 to 4 hours to ripen the ice cream.

Makes 1 1/2 quarts ice cream.

27

Lemon Meringue Pie

THE QUAKERS RECEIVE credit for inventing lemon custard in the late 1700s. Philadelphian Elizabeth Coane Goodfellow, a pastry chef, businesswoman, and cooking school founder, who arrived in Philadelphia in 1806, took lemon custard to another level when she invented lemon meringue pie. Perhaps Lewis sampled his first slice of pie during his return visit in the spring and summer of 1807.

CRUST

3/4 cup all-purpose flour

1/4 cup whole wheat flour

1/4 teaspoon salt

1/4 cup lard or
vegetable shortening

2 to 3 tablespoons
cold water

FILLING

1 1/3 cups sugar

1 cup water

1/4 cup cornstarch

3 eggs, separated

1/4 cup fresh lemon juice

1 tablespoon butter

1/8 teaspoon salt

To make the crust, place the flours and salt in a medium bowl. Cut in the lard with a pastry blender or with 2 knives until the mixture is the size of peas. Sprinkle with water, 1 tablespoon at a time, until the dough holds together. Form into a ball, cover, and chill in the refrigerator for about 20 minutes.

Roll out the dough on a lightly floured surface into a 10- to 11-inch circle. Fold in half and in half again. Gently place in 9-inch baking dish. Unfold and press into dish. Trim and flute edge. Prick the sides and bottom of the crust generously with the tines of a fork to allow air to escape during baking.

Bake at 450°F for 10 to 12 minutes, or until the crust is lightly browned.

Meanwhile, prepare the filling. Combine 1 cup of the sugar and 1/2 cup of the water in a medium saucepan and cook over medium-high heat until the sugar is dissolved, 2 to 3 minutes. Combine the cornstarch and remaining 1/2 cup water in a small bowl. Stir all at once into the hot sugar mixture. Bring to a boil and stir 2 to 3 minutes, or until the mixture is clear and bubbly.

Lemon Meringue Pie, continued

Stir about 1/4 cup hot mixture into the egg yolks and add to saucepan. Cook for 2 to 3 minutes more, or until the mixture is glossy and the eggs are cooked. Remove from the heat. Stir in the lemon juice, butter, and salt. Stir until the butter is melted. Pour the hot filling into the cooled crust.

Place the egg whites in a medium mixer bowl. Beat until foamy. While beating, add 1/3 cup of sugar, 1 tablespoon at a time, and beat until stiff peaks hold. Cover the filling with meringue, sealing the meringue to the edge of the crust over the filling. Place in 350°F oven and bake for 15 minutes, or until the meringue is golden brown. Cool for about 1 hour before serving.

Makes 8 servings.

29

20 June 1803

Jefferson[v]

"The object of your mission is to explore the Missouri river, & such principal stream of it, as, by it is course and communication with the waters of the Pacific ocean, whether the Columbia, Oregan, Colorado or any other river may offer the most direct & practicable water communication across this continent for the purposes of commerce."

President Jefferson's Instructions

THE EXPEDITION FORMED part of Jefferson's grand vision for the United States of America, yet he valued the ordinary details of daily life. The President wanted accurate maps and careful field notes to detail the landscape and all animals, plants, and natural formations. He asked that Lewis extend every courtesy to any people they would meet and to record how they grew crops, fished, and hunted. Jefferson asked Lewis to observe their **"food and domestic accommodations."**

Final Preparations

LEWIS HIRED A horse and driver to carry the 3,500 pounds of supplies by wagon to Pittsburgh. Meanwhile, he returned on horseback to Washington for final instructions from the president and to complete personal and journey business.

In a 2 July 1803 letter to his mother, Lucy Marks, Lewis wrote, **"I go with the most perfect preconviction in my own mind of returning safe and hope therefore that you will not suffer yourself to indulge any anxiety for my safety."**[iv]

Notes

i   *Thomas Jefferson Papers*, Manuscript Division, Library of Congress.

ii Donald Jackson, ed., *Letters of the Lewis and Clark Expedition with Related Documents 1783 –
    1854*, 2 volumes (Urbana: University of Illinois Press, 1978), 1:95-99.

iii Eliza Leslie, *Miss Leslie's Directions for Cookery* (Mineola, New York:
    Dover Publications, 1999).

iv *Letters*, 1:100.

v   *Thomas Jefferson Papers*, Manuscript Division, Library of Congress.

31

PHILADELPHIA
MAY TO JUNE 1803

CHAPTER THREE

Down the Ohio: Pittsburgh to Camp Dubois
30 August 1803 to 13 May 1804

Anticipation and Preparation

IN THE SUMMER of 1803, Lewis arrived by horseback at Pittsburgh, famed for its boat builders. Here, Lewis waited and watched while his barge, the keelboat, was completed. He and his crew loaded the boat and started down the Ohio River on 31 August 1803. Within the next two weeks, they added two pirogues, that Lewis sometimes called canoes.

Newcomers in Wheeling, Cinncinati, and Louisville lived in a sometimes uneasy balance with such native tribes as the Shawnee and the Delaware. The settlers kept cows for cheese and butter and butchered old cows and bulls for meat. They raised pigs for smoked hams, salt pork, and lard. Wheat, corn, and vegetables grew in their fields and gardens. Most hunted to feed their families. Lewis and his crew would eat much the same foods from now until they started the journey up the Missouri.

Kentuckian William Clark, under whom Lewis had served in the U.S. Army during the 1790s, had accepted Lewis's invitation to help command the Expedition. The affable Clark and the more introspective Lewis formed one of the most successful exploration partnerships in American history. Lewis stopped at Clark's hometown, Louisville, to bring aboard Clark and ten young men from Kentucky, including Clark's slave, York, the first African-"American" to explore the lands newly claimed by the United States. The group left from the Falls of the Ohio on 26 October 1803.

Lewis and Clark had Camp Dubois built for their winter lodgings at Wood River, Illinois, on the eastern side of the Mississippi River from St. Louis. The eastern shore ceased to be the western boundary of the United States when the Louisiana Purchase was completed.

Seaman: Hunter Among Hunters

LEWIS WROTE INFREQUENTLY about his Newfoundland, Seaman, but enough that we know the dog was a faithful companion. On 11 September 1803, Seaman plunged into the Ohio River to catch squirrels for Lewis's dinner. **"I made my dog take as many [squirrels] each day as I had occation for, they wer fat and I thought them when fryed a pleasent food,"**[1] wrote Lewis.

Seaman got his rewards when the men gave part of every hunt to him. On 8 May 1806, Lewis wrote that Seaman brought in a deer that one of the men had wounded. When the travelers were hungry, so was Seaman. No doubt the dog also gnawed many meaty buffalo bones.

DOWN THE OHIO: PITTSBURGH TO CAMP DUBOIS
30 AUGUST 1803 TO 13 MAY 1804

34

Honey Black-Walnut Bread

AT WHEELING, VIRGINA (now West Virginia), Lewis looked forward to freshly baked bread. He had directed an unnamed corporal to trade flour with a woman who would bake ninety pounds of bread for them. The corporal and the baker had a disagreement at delivery. The corporal returned to the boats without the bread—and to a displeased Lewis. After a reprimand, Lewis gave him a dollar and told him to go back and get the bread and **"pay the woman for her trouble."**

2 cups boiling water	1/2 cup warm water (120°F)
1/2 cup cracked wheat	1/4 cup honey
3 1/2 cups all-purpose flour	3 tablespoons melted butter
2 cups whole wheat flour	1/2 cup chopped black or English walnuts
4 1/2 teaspoons active dry yeast	
2 teaspoons salt	

Pour 2 cups boiling water over the cracked wheat in a small bowl. Let stand for 20 minutes.

Combine 2 cups of the all-purpose flour, the whole wheat flour, yeast, and salt in a large mixer bowl. Stir in the softened cracked wheat with the soaking water, 1/2 cup warm water, honey, and melted butter. Mix on low speed for 1 minute. Increase the speed to medium and mix for 2 to 3 minutes.

Using the mixer or stirring by hand, add 1 cup all-purpose flour and walnuts, mixing until smooth.

Turn the dough out onto a lightly floured board. Add as much remaining all-purpose flour, 1/4 to 1/2 cup, as needed to leave the dough not sticky. Knead for about 5 minutes, or until the dough is smooth to the touch.

Honey Black-Walnut Bread, continued

Cover with a clean towel and set in a warm place (75° to 80°F) and let the dough rise 50 to 60 minutes, or until doubled in size. Turn the dough out and shape into 2 loaves. Place in well-greased 8 x 4- or 9 x 5-inch bread pans. Let rise another 45 to 50 minutes, or until doubled. Bake in a 375°F oven for 30 to 40 minutes, or until the loaves are lightly browned and sound hollow when thumped.

Makes 2 loaves.

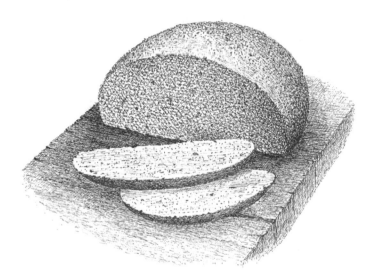

Undated, circa May 1804

Clark[iv]

"...the inhabtents of St. Charles & potage de Scioux had ther crops of corn & wheat. on the upland is a fine farming country partially timbered for Some distance back."

35

Pan-Roasted Apple Butter

TRIBAL PEOPLE HAD long collected wild fruits and preserved them by drying. Settlers picked fruit both wild and from orchards they planted and tended to make jams, jellies and steeped fruit (see Brandied Spiced Peaches, page 7).

3 pounds apples, such as Granny Smith, Jonathan, Winesap, Wealthy, Golden Delicious, or McIntosh, unpeeled, cored, and coarsely chopped (about 6 medium apples)

3 cups (firmly packed) brown sugar

I teaspoon ground cinnamon

I/2 teaspoon ground nutmeg

I/2 teaspoon ground cloves

I/8 teaspoon salt

Combine all the ingredients in a 3-quart saucepan. Bring to a boil over medium-high heat for 20 minutes. Reduce the heat to medium-low. Cook, uncovered, for about 1 1/2 hours, stirring frequently, until the apples are very tender and the liquid is thickened and syrupy.

Remove from the heat and let cool for 10 minutes. Place small batches of apples with liquid in a food processor or blender. Process until the mixture is smooth and thick.

Pour into clean jars (four I-cup jars or two I-pint jars) with tight-fitting lids. Use immediately or refrigerate for up to 1 month or freeze for up to 6 months.

Makes 4 cups apple butter.

Pan-Fried Potatoes

SETTLERS IN THE Wood River area no doubt had been growing potatoes (*Solanum tuberosum*) for some time. The vegetable originated in the central Andes where the Incas grew potatoes for food and for medicine and wove them into their social traditions from around 200 B.C. The tuber's value was not lost on the sixteenth-century Spanish explorers, who sent potatoes back to Europe to be cultivated. By the early 1800s, settlers and soldiers on the American frontier knew and grew potatoes as a familiar food with European origins, especially linked to Ireland.

From the earliest days of the trip, Lewis and Clark observed and ate wild roots. Lewis wrote from the lower Missouri about a water lily variety (*Nymphaea tuberosa*), the prairie turnip (*Pediomelum esculentum*), a lotus (*Nelumbo lutea*), and the groundnut (*Apios americana*). They observed these plants with interest. Later in the Northwest, native roots and the skills for selecting and preparing them would provide their food salvation (see pages 109, 114, 127). Lewis and Clark often compared unfamiliar roots to those they knew: the common potato, sweet potato (*Ipomaea batatas*), and carrot (*Daucus carota sativa*).

2 pounds potatoes (about 6 medium potatoes)	1/4 cup butter
Salt	1/2 teaspoon freshly ground black pepper

Peel the potatoes and place them in cold water with 1 teaspoon salt per 4 cups water until all the potatoes are peeled. This helps keep the potatoes from discoloring before they are cooked.

Melt the butter in a skillet over medium heat. Remove the skillet from the heat. Thinly slice the potatoes, rinsing each as you remove it from the soaking water. Layer the potatoes in the skillet and toss with pepper and 1 teaspoon salt. Toss to coat well with butter. Return the pan to the heat. Cook over medium to medium-low heat for 30 to 35 minutes, turning the potatoes as they brown. Serve immediately.

Makes 6 to 8 servings.

Molasses Baked Beans

PEOPLE OF EUROPEAN descent did not hesitate to add beans, native to the Americas, to their gardens. They adapted dried bean cookery to their own tastes, adding such ingredients as ham, bacon, and sweeteners. Philadelphia and St. Louis merchants imported sugar and molasses from Caribbean plantations worked by African slaves. Baked beans remain an early example of global fusion cooking.

The recipe requires no pre-soaking for the dried beans.

1 pound dried navy beans	3 tablespoons molasses
1 medium onion, peeled and chopped	2 teaspoons dry mustard
	1/2 pound bacon, chopped
1 cup sugar	1/2 pound ham, chopped

Rinse and drain the beans. Combine the beans, onion, sugar, molasses, dry mustard, and 5 cups of water in a cooking pot and cover with foil and a tight lid. Place in a 300°F oven and bake for 7 to 10 hours, stirring every 1 1/2 hours. After the first 3 hours, stir in the bacon and ham. Continue stirring every 1 1/2 hours and cook until the beans are tender. If necessary, add up to 2 cups water, 1/2 cup at a time, to keep the beans moist. Serve immediately or refrigerate or freeze.

To reheat, add 1 to 2 tablespoons water per cup of prepared beans.

Makes 12 to 14 servings.

Succotash with Cream

NARRAGANSETT, HURON, AND many other tribal people who grew corn had been eating mixed corn and beans long before the first recorded mention of succotash in a New England August 1751 diary entry. The word succotash is said to come from a Narragansett word, *msiquatash*. The dish remains popular among the Narragansett of Rhode Island.

This is one of many versions of succotash found across the United States, one that settlers around St. Louis may have made.

2 cups whole kernel corn, fresh or frozen

2 cups cooked lima beans, fresh or frozen

3 to 4 tablespoons half-and-half

1/4 to 1/2 teaspoon salt

1/4 teaspoon freshly ground black pepper

Combine the corn and beans in a medium saucepan. Add about 1/2 cup water. Bring to a boil. Reduce the heat to low. Simmer for about 10 minutes, allowing the water to evaporate.

With a slotted spoon, drain and remove the vegetables to a serving dish. Pour the half-and-half over the top and sprinkle with salt and pepper. Toss together lightly. Serve immediately.

Makes 6 to 8 servings.

39

25 February 1804

Clark to his brother Jonathan[v]

"Dear Brother, we dined as yesterday with the Lt. Govr. a most Sumpcious Dinner, & a large Company. a great Deel of formality and parade was displayed...."

St. Louis Apple Tart

THE LOUISIANA PURCHASE effectively moved the central United States from western Virginia to the St. Louis area and transposed the western frontier to the Rocky Mountains. The French had founded the city in 1764. Over the next fifty years, St. Louis cooks mingled native and imported foods with French, Spanish, and Northern European food traditions.

The apple (*Malus pumila*) adapted well from Europe to North America, as did wheat (*Triticum sp.*). St. Louis imported other ingredients from Philadelphia via the Ohio River and the overland Natchez Trace.

Country cooks have long preferred lard for the flakiest piecrust. Feel free to substitute shortening or use all butter in this rustic dessert.

1 cup all-purpose flour

1/2 cup stone-ground cornmeal

1/2 teaspoon salt

1/4 cup plus 1/3 cup butter

1/4 cup lard or hydrogenated shortening

3 to 4 tablespoons cold water

2 pounds apples, such as Granny Smith, Jonathan, Winesap, Wealthy, Golden Delicious, or McIntosh, peeled, cored, and thinly sliced (about 4 to 6 medium apples)

1/2 cup plus 2 tablespoons (firmly packed) brown sugar

1/2 teaspoon ground cinnamon

1/2 teaspoon grated lemon zest

Mix the flour, cornmeal, and salt in a medium bowl. With a pastry blender or with 2 knives, cut in the 1/4 cup butter and the lard until the mixture is the size of shelled peas. Add the water, 1 tablespoon at a time, and stir until the dough holds together. Chill about 20 minutes.

St. Louis Apple Tart, continued

Meanwhile, melt the 1/2 cup brown sugar, 1/3 cup butter, and the cinnamon in an ovenproof 9- or 10-inch skillet. Arrange the apple slices in the pan and cook over medium heat for about 15 minutes, stirring occasionally, until tender.

Mix 2 tablespoons brown sugar and the lemon zest. Sprinkle over the apples. Roll out the dough on a lightly floured surface to a 9- or 10-inch circle. Lay over the apples.

Bake in a 375°F oven for about 30 minutes, or until the crust is golden brown. Loosen around the edge of the tart with a clean knife. Place a large, round platter on top of the pan. Invert quickly to let the tart slide from the pan. Serve warm or chilled.

Makes 8 servings.

Lewis[vi]

Detachment
Orders

*"The four men who are
engaged in making sugar
[tapping sugar maples]
will continue in that
employment untill further
orders, and will recieve
each a half a gill of extra
whiskey pr. day and be
exempt from guard duty."*

Ardent Spirits

THE UNITED STATES Army issued whiskey as standard procedure, as had armies for centuries. These rations were not only a pleasant diversion, but a tool of reward and discipline. On 20 February 1804, Lewis's men received an extra half gill, or two fluid ounces, for their work. Later on the Expedition, John Collins broke into the whiskey stores and shared some with Hugh Hall. As 29 June 1804 dawned, the men, now drunk, were arrested and brought to trial. Collins received 100 lashes and Hall, 50.

The daily whiskey ration was a gill, about four ounces. Lewis granted his men two gills, one cup, on his 1804 birthday on the Middle Missouri. By 4 July 1805, the captains issued the last spirits for rations, but saved a store for medicinal purposes (see page 98).

Cornmeal Mush with Cheese

If Hoe Cakes (see page 56) shows one of the simplest ways to enjoy cornmeal, Cornmeal Mush with Cheese is its sophisticated cousin. You will still find it, called Cheese Grits, on restaurant menus and in homes throughout the South.

2/3 cup white or yellow
stone-ground cornmeal

1/2 teaspoon salt

1 cup grated mild cheese,
such as mild Cheddar or Colby
(1/4 pound cheese)

2 tablespoons butter

Butter or preferred
fat for frying

Mix the cornmeal, salt, and 2 cups of water in a medium saucepan over medium-high heat. Bring to a boil, stirring constantly. Reduce the heat and cook for 7 to 10 minutes, stirring constantly to keep the mixture smooth.

When thickened, remove from the heat and stir in the cheese and butter. Serve immediately or place in a greased 9-inch square baking dish and chill in the refrigerator. Slice and fry in hot butter until golden brown.

Makes 9 servings.

43

Hominy Fritters

BESIDES BEEF, PORK, and wild game, the men at Camp Dubois ate plenty of cornmeal and hominy, milk, and eggs. While baking powder was not invented until 1856, early nineteenth-century cooks sometimes used pearl ash, a baking powder forerunner, to leaven and lighten quick breads, biscuits, and fritters.

1 cup whole wheat flour	2 eggs, well beaten
1 cup all-purpose flour	2/3 cup milk
1 tablespoon baking powder	1 cup rinsed and drained hominy
1 tablespoon sugar	Vegetable oil, for frying
1/4 teaspoon salt	Honey or syrup, for serving

Combine the flours, baking powder, sugar, and salt in a medium bowl. Stir in the eggs and milk, just until ingredients are mixed. Stir in the hominy to blend evenly. Batter will be lumpy. Take care not to overstir, or the fritters will be tough.

Heat about 2 inches of vegetable oil to 365°F in a large, heavy saucepan. Spoon a scant 2 tablespoons of fritter batter into the hot oil, cooking no more than 3 fritters at a time. Fry about 2 minutes on each side. Skim and remove any crumbs after each batch. Serve hot with honey or syrup.

Makes 14 to 18 fritters.

Homemade Hominy

THOUGH THE WORD for hominy comes from the Algonquian, the practice of soaking some of the corn crop in wood ashes or lime dates back to the Aztecs and the Mayans. Most tribes who grew corn in the late eighteenth and early nineteenth centuries prepared hominy. The caustic alkaline solution dissolved the tough skin over corn kernels, making it easier to chew and digest. Contemporary science has determined that the process both raises the available protein and releases niacin otherwise not absorbed during digestion.

Commercially canned hominy, either white or yellow, is available across the country and easy to find in the American South and in Hispanic markets. Rinse it well before using.

The quality of homemade hominy depends on the kind of corn (large-kerneled dent corn is good), the kind of wood ash available, or, if using, the lime or lye made for human consumption.

2 cups dried unparched corn kernels	1/4 cup powdered lime or 1/2 cup wood ashes (ash, cottonwood, cedar, but not from chemically treated wood)

Soak the corn kernels in 4 cups of water overnight. Stir in the lime or ashes. Bring to a boil. Reduce the heat and simmer, covered, for 2 to 2 1/2 hours, or until the hulls have loosened. The dryness of the corn determines the cooking time.

Remove from the heat and let soak overnight. Wash the corn under cool water to remove the ash and hulls. Cover the cleaned kernels with water. Bring to a boil. Reduce the heat and simmer, covered, 1 to 2 hours, or until the kernels are tender.

28 March 1804

Clark[viii]

"I had Corn parched to make parched meal...."

Indian Pudding

NATIVE TRIBES FROM the Northeast to the Southwest had long prepared ground cornmeal into puddings, stews, and cakes. Newly arrived Europeans added cornmeal to their own puddings, which were often rich in eggs, milk, and spices.

4 cups milk

1/2 cup stone-ground cornmeal

3 eggs

1/4 cup molasses

1/4 cup (firmly packed) brown sugar

1/2 teaspoon ground cinnamon

1/2 teaspoon ground nutmeg

1/2 teaspoon salt

3 to 4 tablespoons butter

Beat together 3 cups of the milk and the cornmeal. Bring to a boil. Reduce the heat to medium and stir constantly for about 15 minutes, or until the mixture is thickened. Pour into a well-greased 1 1/2-quart casserole. Beat together the eggs, molasses, brown sugar, cinnamon, nutmeg, and salt. Stir gently, but thoroughly, into cornmeal mixture. Dot with butter. Slowly pour the remaining cup of milk evenly over the top.

Bake in a 300°F oven for about 2 1/2 hours, or until the mixture is set.

Makes about 6 servings.

46

Hunters

THE EXPEDITION HUNTERS did their best to supply the Corps with what they most wanted to eat: meat. It is recorded that at times, the men ate up to nine pounds of meat a day, meat that was much leaner than most meat available commercially today.

At Camp Dubois and later on the journey, the Corps often traded with tribal hunters for meat. When buffalo was plentiful, Corps members ate their fill. If the hunters shot a wolf, they ate it. If the hunt yielded squirrels or opossums, the Corps ate them. In May 1805, they measured 6 gallons of fat and 400 pounds of meat from a bear whose head, alone, measured 3 feet 5 inches around.

Animal fat was equally important to keeping the group relatively healthy and nourished. Fat provides more than twice as many calories per ounce as either meat protein or the carbohydrates in roots, other vegetables, and fruits. Calories mattered to men laboring through a cold winter to prepare for the trip and later pulling pirogues and a keelboat against a five-mile-per-hour current up the Missouri River.

18 December 1803

Clark to his brother, Jonathan[ix]

"Dear Brother, we met with a great many Showonee Indians and traded with them for different kinds of wild meets, Such as Biar, Vensions, Ducs, Tongues, and Beaver Tales..."

19 January 1804

Clark[x]

"Gibson Killed 3 Deer & Colter 3 Turkey, Shields 4 Turkey, Worne[r] & Thompson"

47

Grill-Roasted Turkey with Sausage Stuffing

LEWIS FIRST NOTED a turkey shot on 1 September 1803. The hunter brought in turkey again for Christmas. Plump domestic twenty-first-century turkeys do not resemble wild turkeys, either those of 1803 or of the present. Wild animals choose their own diet, unlike farm-raised animals that eat what they are offered.

One 12-pound domestic turkey, fresh or frozen

1 pound ground pork or ground pork-ground beef mixture

1 tablespoon fresh marjoram leaves, chopped, or 1 teaspoon dried marjoram leaves

1/2 teaspoon salt

1/2 teaspoon freshly ground black pepper

1/4 teaspoon ground nutmeg

4 cups bread cubes from dense bread such as sourdough

1 tablespoon butter

If frozen, thaw the turkey according to package directions. Remove the giblets and rinse bird inside and out. If desired, simmer the giblets in about 1 cup water in a small saucepan for about 10 minutes. Drain and chop the giblets and reserve the broth or prepare about 3/4 cup chicken broth.

Combine the ground pork, marjoram, salt, pepper, and nutmeg. Mix well. Toss in the bread cubes and stir in 1/3 cup of reserved broth. Add additional broth by the tablespoon until all the bread pieces are just moist but not mushy.

Grill-Roasted Turkey with Sausage Stuffing, continued

Loosely stuff the cavity and the neck. Close with metal or bamboo skewers. Place the remaining stuffing in a greased 1-quart casserole dish.

Place the turkey in a large roaster pan. Brush with melted butter.

Preheat the grill to 450°F or very hot. Place the turkey roaster on the grill. Adjust the coals or controls to lower the heat to 350°F. Cover the grill. Check the temperature level after 15 minutes. After 15 minutes more, pour 1/4 cup additional broth over turkey. Continue to add coals or adjust controls to maintain the heat at 350°F. Roast for about 3 hours, or 15 minutes per pound. Begin testing the turkey with an instant-read meat thermometer at 2 1/2 hours. Turkey is safely cooked when the juices run clear and the thermometer registers 170°F in the breast or 180°F in the thickest part of the thigh.

Bake the extra stuffing, uncovered, alongside the turkey for the last 50 minutes, or until stuffing is bubbly and lightly browned. If there is not room on the grill, bake in a 350°F oven for about 50 minutes.

Remove the turkey from the grill and leave in the roaster at room temperature, loosely covered with aluminum foil, for about 20 minutes. Spoon the stuffing from the cavity into a serving bowl. Carve the turkey and serve.

Makes about 24 servings

TO ROAST IN THE OVEN: Prepare the turkey as directed. Heat the oven to 450°F. Place the turkey roaster in the oven and lower the heat to 350°F. Continue as above.

1 January 1804

Clark[xii]

"Several men Come from the Countrey to See us & Shoot with the men, they bring Sugare &c. to trade, I purchase Sugar 6 lb. at 1/6 per pound.... A Perogue Passed Loaded with Salt & Dry goods. Jos: Vaun offers to let the Contrator have Beef at 4$ pd. or 3$ 50 Cents in money."

3 January, 1804

Clark[xiii]

"Comy [commissary] Kiled a Beef..."

Roast Beef with Mashed Potatoes

IN ADDITION TO hunting wild animals for meat, the Corps bought cattle from local farmers.

1 to 2 tablespoons fat (beef suet, lard, butter, or vegetable oil)

One 2- to 3-pound beef rump, chuck, or bottom round roast

MASHED POTATOES

4 medium potatoes, peeled and quartered

1/4 cup warm milk

Salt and pepper to taste

ROASTED VEGETABLES

3 medium potatoes, peeled and quartered

6 medium carrots, peeled and cut in half crosswise

1 medium onion, peeled and cut into quarters

Heat the fat and brown the meat on all sides in a 3-quart roaster over medium to medium-high heat for about 5 minutes. Pour 1/2 cup water over the meat. Bring to a boil. Reduce the heat to medium-low. Simmer, covered, for 2 1/2 to 3 hours, or until tender.

To prepare the mashed potatoes, place the potatoes in a saucepan and cover with water. Boil for about 30 minutes, or until the potatoes are tender. Drain. Pour the milk over the potatoes. Mash by hand or with an electric mixer until the potatoes are smooth. Add salt and pepper to taste. During the last 30 minutes of braising, arrange the mashed potatoes around the roast. To serve, slice the meat and serve with the potatoes.

If you prefer to roast the meat with vegetables, arrange the vegetables around the roast during the last hour of braising. Remove the meat and carve. Place on a platter with the mashed potatoes or with the roasted vegetables.

Makes 6 to 8 servings.

Anticipation

ANYONE WHO HAS planned a family trip or a wilderness canoe adventure knows that moment when you check to see if everything is in order. The next moment, ready or not, it is time to depart. Captains Lewis and Clark had made their preparations. None of that guaranteed their success or their safety.

1 April 1804

Clark[xiv]

"The Camp Kittles, and other Public utensels for Cooking Shall be produced this evening after the parade is Dismissed; and an equal division shall take place of the Same.... each [of three] squad[s] shall be devided into two messes...."

2 April 1804

Clark[xv]

"I have meal mad & the flour Packed & repacked, also Some porkie packed in barrels, a Windey Day"

51

[i] Meriwether Lewis and William Clark, *The Journals of the Lewis and Clark Expedition*, 13 volumes, ed. Gary E. Moulton (Lincoln, Nebraska: University of Nebraska Press, 1983–2001). Lewis, 2:79.

[ii] Ibid., 2:75.

[iii] Ibid., Clark, 2:181.

[iv] Ibid., 2:218-19.

[v] William Clark, *Dear Brother: Letters of William Clark to Jonathan Clark*, ed. James J. Holmberg (New Haven: Yale University Press, 2002). 77.

[vi] *Journals*, Lewis, 2:175.

[vii] Ibid., Clark, 2:173.

[viii] Ibid., 2:181.

[ix] Clark, *Dear Brother*, 61.

[x] *Journals*, Clark, 2:158.

[xi] Ibid., 2:140-41.

[xii] Ibid., 2:144.

[xiii] Ibid., 2:145.

[xiv] Ibid., 2:189.

[xv] Ibid., 2:191.

CHAPTER FOUR

Upstream on the Missouri
14 May to 20 August 1804

High Spirits

ON 14 MAY 1804, Clark left Camp Dubois commanding the crews of the well-loaded keelboat and the two pirogues. **"Men in high Spirits,"** he wrote. The command paddled upriver to St. Charles to wait for Lewis to arrive from St. Louis.

A week later, more than forty men left St. Charles, including at least twenty-five of the people who would complete the journey. Extra boatmen signed on to row and pull the pirogues and the keelboat, weighted with more than 14,000 pounds of supplies. Well-wishers sent them off with three cheers.

The captains must have been mindful of President Jefferson's instructions as well as their own hopes for success. They tended, as well, to such practical matters as food rations, guard duty, and keeping order among the command, all marks of the military expedition that it was.

List of Provisions: [i]

A Memorandum of Articles in Readiness for the Voyage [partial listing]

		WT. [POUNDS]
[do = ditto]		
14	Bags of Parchmeal of 2 bus: each about	1200
9	do Common Do do do	800
11	do Corn Hulled do do	1000
30 half Barrels of flour 3 Bags of do	} +1 (Gross 3900w) do	3400
7 do of Biscuit 4 Barrels of do	} +1 (Gross 650) do	560
7	Barrels of Salt of 2 bus: each " (870) do	750
50	Kegs of Pork (gross 4500) do	3705
2	Boxes of Candles 70 lb and about 50 lb (one of which has 50 lb of soap[)] do	170
1	Bag of Candle-wick do	8
1 do	Coffee	50
1 do	Beens & 1 of Peas	100
2 do	Sugar do	112
1	Keg of Hogs Lard do	100
4	Barrels of Corn hulled (650) do	600
1	do of meal (170) do	150

600 lb Grees

50 bushels meal

24 do Natchies Corn Huled

21 Bales of Indians goods

Tools of every Description & &.

26 May 1804

Lewis[ii]

From Detachment Orders:

"Sergt. John Ordway will continue to issue the provisions and make the detales for guard or other duty. The day after tomorrow lyed corn and grece will be issued to the party, the next day Poark and flour, and the day following Indian meal and poark; and in conformity to that ratiene provisions will continue to be issued to the party untill further orders. should any of the messes prefer indian meal to flour they may recieve it accordingly— no poark is to be issued when we have fresh meat on hand."

Provisions Pork Stew

PORK WAS THE single largest food item packed for the journey. The Corps carried 3,705 pounds, almost two tons, of pork layered into 50 kegs, plus a 100-pound keg of lard. For the next few months, if the hunters did not come back with wild game, the Corps ate pork.

Europeans introduced the pig to the American continent. Small farmers kept pigs and continued the northern European tradition of smoking hams and sausage, foods that kept well without modern refrigeration.

2 pounds pork butt, well trimmed and cut into 1 1/2-inch cubes

1/4 cup stone-ground cornmeal

1 teaspoon salt

1/2 teaspoon freshly ground black pepper

2 to 3 tablespoons salt pork or vegetable oil

2 onions, peeled and cut into eighths

4 cups beef broth

Cornmeal Dumplings (recipe follows)

Place the pork in a paper bag with the cornmeal, salt, and pepper. Close and shake to dredge the pork.

Heat the salt pork in large pot. Lightly brown the pork cubes on all sides. Stir in the onions and cook until they soften.

Pour in the beef broth. Simmer over medium-low heat for about 1 hour. For best flavor, cool and refrigerate the stew overnight.

The next day, skim the fat from the surface. Bring to a boil and lower the heat. Cook for at least 20 minutes, stirring often. Do not allow the bottom to burn. Meanwhile, prepare the dumplings.

Makes 4 to 6 servings.

Cornmeal Dumplings

STEAMED BATTER CAKES, known as dumplings, fall somewhere between a biscuit and a pudding. For best results, spoon them gently on the stew and resist removing the cover until the end of cooking time.

1 cup all-purpose flour	1/2 teaspoon salt
1/4 cup stone-ground yellow cornmeal	1 tablespoon vegetable oil, melted butter, or fat of your choice
1 teaspoon baking powder	

Mix the flour, cornmeal, baking powder, and salt. Stir in 1/3 cup of water and the oil, just until the mixture is moistened. Excess stirring will make dumplings tough.

Gently drop spoonfuls of dough on top of the stew while it is simmering over medium-high heat. Cover the pan tightly. Lower the heat to medium-low and cook the dumplings for about 10 minutes without lifting the cover during cooking. Serve immediately.

Makes 6 to 8 dumplings.

UPSTREAM ON THE MISSOURI
14 MAY TO 20 AUGUST 1804

28 May 1804

Lewis[iii]

From Detachment Orders:

"provision for one day will be issued to the party on each evening after we have encamped; the same will be cooked on that evening by the several messes, and a proportion of it reserved for the next day as no cooking will be allowed in the day while on the mach [march]"

Hoe Cakes

HOE CAKES (also called corn pone) got its name from early settlers who cooked their corn patties on the metal blade of a hoe over an open fire. Native Americans had been preparing corn cakes for hundreds of years, an idea readily adopted by Europeans. The Expedition packed twelve hundred pounds of parched meal plus another fifty bushels.

Use fresh stone-ground cornmeal and you may be surprised at how much flavor is packed in this simple recipe. Culinary historian John Egerton says, "The flavor is from fat and salt. You can't have too much grease."

I cup stone-ground cornmeal

1/8 to 1/4 teaspoon salt

1/2 to 3/4 cup boiling water

I tablespoon fat or more (butter, oil, beef suet, lard, or your choice)

Combine the cornmeal and salt in a small bowl. Stir in 1/2 cup boiling water. Stir well. Test to see if the mixture holds its shape without crumbling. If necessary, add more boiling water, I tablespoon at a time. Form the mixture, 2 or 3 tablespoonfuls at a time, into a 3-inch circle, 1/2 to 3/4 inch thick.

Heat the fat in a heavy skillet over medium-high heat. Reduce the heat to medium. Place the patties in the hot fat and pat lightly with a spatula. Fry for I minute on each side.

Makes 6 servings.

Everyday Hominy with Bacon

CANNED, COOKED HOMINY is a modern convenience in this version of the Expedition rations of **"lyed corn and greece."**

Noted cookbook author Edna Lewis has written that cooked hominy reminds her of small dumplings.

1 can (14 1/2 ounces) yellow hominy	1 medium onion, peeled and chopped
1 can (14 1/2 ounces) white hominy	1/4 teaspoon freshly ground pepper
1/4 pound bacon, chopped	

Drain the hominy and rinse well under cool water. Set aside. Cook the bacon in a heavy skillet over medium heat until almost crisp, 5 to 7 minutes. If desired, remove all but 1 tablespoon of the bacon fat. Stir in the onion and cook over medium heat for about 4 minutes, or until the onion is softened. Stir in the hominy, 1/4 cup of water, and the pepper. Cook over medium heat for about 10 minutes, or until the hominy is cooked through and the flavors are blended. Serve immediately.

Makes about 8 servings.

Mealtime

THE CORPS HAD a hot meal once a day. For breakfast and lunch, the travelers ate the leftovers. Many dishes were cooked in the six brass kettles that Lewis had bought in Philadelphia (see page 16). The open-fire cooking style during the journey differed little from that at Camp Dubois, in ocean-going ships, or even the open hearths in all but the wealthiest homes on the continent. In the late 1700s, physicist Benjamin Rumford had invented the cast-iron cookstove. The innovation began to be widely available after 1815.

One day York added some variety to the captains' menu.

5 June 1804

Clark[iv]

"here my Servant York Swam to the Sand bar to geather greens for our Dinner and returnd with a Sufficent quantity wild Creases or Teng grass."

Greens with Salt Pork

MUCH OF THE cooking in the captains' squad may have fallen to York, Clark's slave. As the Expedition moved west, the journals reveal that York was treated more as a member of the command and less as the property of another man. Tribal people noticed his skin color and his strength.

1 pound fresh spinach or other greens

1/4 to 1/2 pound salt pork, diced

1/4 teaspoon freshly ground black pepper

Rinse the spinach well in cool water and pat it dry. Cook the salt pork in a large heavy saucepan over medium heat for 4 to 5 minutes. Add the spinach and pepper, tossing gently to mix with the salt pork. Stir in 1 to 2 tablespoons water, 1 tablespoon at a time. Steam the spinach, covered, over medium heat about 5 minutes, stirring occasionally, or until the greens have wilted. Serve immediately.

Makes 4 servings.

Butter Island Spoon Bread

19 July 1804
Clark

"I call this Island Butter
Island, as at this place
we mad use of the last
of our butter."

EXPEDITION MEMBERS LEFT many comforts behind. To think of Clark savoring the last of the butter is to imagine him letting go of one more.

2/3 cup white or yellow stone-ground cornmeal

1/2 teaspoon salt

2 cups milk or water

4 eggs

3 tablespoons butter

1 tablespoon baking powder

Cinnamon sugar, for serving

Stir the cornmeal and salt into the milk in a medium saucepan. Bring to a boil, stirring constantly. Reduce the heat and cook for 5 to 10 minutes, stirring constantly to keep the mixture smooth.

Beat the eggs. Stir 1/2 cup of the hot cornmeal mixture into the eggs. Stir in the butter. Add the egg-butter mixture to the cornmeal. Beat well. Stir in the baking powder.

Pour into a well-greased baking dish, either a 9-inch square dish or two 9 x 5-inch loaf pans. Bake at 400°F for about 30 minutes, or until the mixture is set. Serve immediately. Good with cinnamon sugar.

Makes 9 to 12 servings.

59

60

White Catfish with Bacon

THE EXPEDITION CAUGHT and ate either the blue catfish (*Ictalurus furcatus*) or the channel catfish (*Ictalurus punctatus*). If it was the latter, Lewis and Clark were the first to record the existence of the channel catfish for Western science. The catfish gets its feline name from the whisker-like feelers the catfish uses to find its food on the river bottom.

2 pounds catfish (4 to 6 fillets)	1/8 to 1/4 teaspoon cayenne
1/2 cup stone-ground cornmeal	6 slices thick-cut bacon (about 1/2 pound)
3/4 teaspoon salt	Vegetable oil or fat of your choice, for frying (optional)
1/4 teaspoon freshly ground black pepper	

Rinse the catfish and shake off excess water. Dredge the fillets in a mixture of cornmeal, salt, pepper, and cayenne. Fry the bacon in a heavy skillet over medium-high heat until slightly crisp. Remove the bacon and set aside. Reduce the heat to medium and add the fillets, frying 2 to 3 minutes on each side, starting with the skin side up. You may need to fry in 2 batches. If necessary, add another tablespoon of oil. Crumble the bacon over the fillets and serve immediately.

Makes 4 to 6 servings.

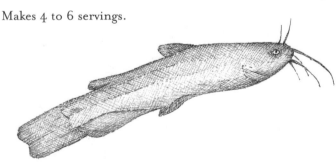

Grilled Mussels

THE CORPS ALSO gathered mussels in June 1805, shortly before leaving the Missouri River. According to Gary Moulton, editor of *The Journals of the Lewis and Clark Expedition*, these were either *Margaritiferidae* or *Unionidae*. In October 1805, Clark recorded seeing mounds of mussel shells along the Columbia River's banks.

Buy only mussels that are tightly sealed. If they have opened before you cook them, they are not fresh. Create smoky flavor over a gas grill by adding soaked wood chips during grilling.

3 pounds fresh mussels, scrubbed and debearded	Salt and freshly ground black pepper

Heat a charcoal grill until hot. Place the mussels on the grill rack in a single layer (do this in batches as necessary); cover the grill and cook 3 to 4 minutes, or just until the mussels open.

Serve the mussels warm, seasoned with salt and pepper.

Makes 6 servings.

Clark[viii]

"I took ten men... and with a Brush Drag caught 308 fish, of the following kind (i'e) Pike, Samon, Bass, Pirch, Red horse, Small Cat, & a kind of Perch Called the Ohio Silverfish. I also Caught the Srimp which is Common to the Lower part of the Mississippi, in this Creek & in the Beaver Pond is emince beads of Mustles Verry large & fat."

61

1 August 1804

Clark[ix]

William Clark's
Birthday

*"3 Deer & an Elk Killed
to day. This being my
birth day I order'd a
Saddle of fat Vennison,
an Elk fleece & a
Bevertail to be cooked
and a Desert of Cheries,
Plumbs, Raspberries
Currents and grapes
of a Supr. quality."*

62

William Clark's Birthday Fruit Salad

THE MEN MAY have mixed fruit into their whiskey to extend their supply to make it last until 4 July 1805 (see page 98).

2 cups fresh grapes
(red, green, or a
combination), halved

I cup pitted cherries,
fresh or frozen

I cup raspberries,
fresh or frozen

I cup fresh plums,
quartered and pitted

I/2 cup fresh currants

I/4 cup whiskey or brandy

Ice cream, pound cake,
or shortcake, for serving

Mix together the grapes, cherries, raspberries, plums, and currants. Toss lightly with the whiskey. Chill in the refrigerator for about I hour. Serve alone or over ice cream, pound cake, or shortcake.

Makes 8 to IO servings.

Birthdays

WILLIAM CLARK WROTE light-hearted entries to mark the captains' August 1804 birthdays. Clark was thirty-four and Lewis, thirty. The next year, Clark does not mention his birthday in the 1 August 1805 entry. Lewis wrote one of the longest introspective commentaries found in the journals on his 18 August 1805 birthday, lamenting time **"spent in indolence."** He resolves **"in the future to live for *mankind* as I have heretofore lived *for myself."*** [x]

On 1 August 1806, Clark was leading part of the Expedition along the Yellowstone River. Again, he does not note his birthday in any way. On 18 August 1806, Lewis no longer made journal entries, although it is a fair guess that the captain was not in a mood to celebrate his birthday. A week earlier, Pierre Cruzatte, the boatman and fiddler with poor eyesight, had confused Lewis with an elk and shot him in the left buttock.

18 August 1804

Clark [xi]

Meriwether Lewis's Birthday

"the evening was Closed with an extra Gill of Whiskey & a Dance untill 11 oClock."

63

On a Somber Note

ON 20 AUGUST 1804, Sergeant Charles Floyd died, probably of the complications of a ruptured appendix at what is now Sioux City, Iowa. The Corps honored him and marked his grave with a cedar post. A one-hundred-foot tall obelisk resembling the Washington Monument in shape was placed in Floyd's memory during the Lewis and Clark Expedition Centennial. Following Floyd's death, Patrick Gass received a promotion to Sergeant, to join Sergeants Nathaniel Pryor and John Ordway. On the return in 1806, the Expedition stopped to pay their respects to Floyd, whose life was the only one the Corps lost during the Expedition.

i Meriwether Lewis and William Clark, *The Journals of the Lewis and Clark Expedition*, 13 volumes, ed. Gary E. Moulton (Lincoln, Nebraska: University of Nebraska Press, 1983–2001). Clark, 2:217-18.

ii Ibid., Lewis, 2:258.

iii Ibid.

iv Ibid., Clark, 2:279.

v Ibid., 2:395.

vi Ibid., 2:418.

vii Ibid., 2:426.

viii Ibid., 2:483.

ix Ibid., 2:433.

x Ibid., Lewis, 5:118.

xi Ibid., Clark, 2:489.

Notes

UPSTREAM ON THE MISSOURI
14 MAY TO 20 AUGUST 1804

Chapter Five

Middle Missouri
21 August to 25 October 1804

Buffalo! Diplomacy with the Yankton and Teton Sioux

United States population in 1804: 5.4 million
Buffalo population in 1804: est. 40 to 75 million

THE EXPEDITION HAD for some time been expecting a major menu change. They had seen signs of buffalo as early as 7 June 1804 and saw the first animals on 28 June 1804. Joseph Fields shot the first buffalo (*Bos bison*) on 23 August 1804.

For the next ten months, the men ate buffalo as often as possible. A single adult buffalo provided up to four hundred pounds of meat, more than enough for the men to eat nine pounds each at some meals.

Even more central to the Expedition's success, they had entered lands where the Sioux Indians lived and hunted, a tribe that the president had singled out in his instructions. Jefferson knew that relations with the Sioux, especially the Teton Sioux who controlled much of the land around the central Missouri River, determined whether European Americans would be able to travel freely in his envisioned West.

On 29 August 1804, the Captains smoked a peace pipe with the Yankton Sioux, who welcomed the visitors and made a feast for them. On 25 September 1804, the Expedition met and shared food and whiskey with the Teton Sioux in what is now central South Dakota. The visit's tone deteriorated and both sides drew their arms. However, no shots or arrows were fired. The Expedition left quickly.

Wild Grapes and a Rabbit

PRIVATE GEORGE SHANNON went missing on 26 August 1804. For the next sixteen days, Expedition members searched for him. On 11 September 1804, the group caught up to him, not knowing he was ahead of them. He had run out of bullets and abandoned one of his horses. For twelve days, Shannon had eaten nothing but wild grapes and did manage to shoot a rabbit using a stick as ammunition. Clark observed, **"thus a man had like to have Starved to death in a land of Plenty for the want of Bulletes or Something to kill his meat."** [i]

MIDDLE MISSOURI
21 AUGUST TO 25 OCTOBER 1804

"I Saw & eat Pemitigon
*[pemmican]... I also
Saw a Spoon made of
a horn of an animile of
the Sheep kind the spoon
will hold 2 quarts."*

68

Jerky: Buffalo, Elk, or Vension

ALTHOUGH THE WORD "jerky" is believed to come from the Spanish *charqui*, meat jerky probably goes back to about the same time as hunters discovered fire. Traditionally, people relied on smoke alone to develop the meat's flavor and color and to preserve it. Smoke also helped keep the flies away. At some point, someone figured out that salt added flavor and made the meat taste better longer. Smoking meat over a wood fire still makes the best jerky.

Buffalo, elk (*Cervus elaphus*), and venison (*Odocoileus sp.*) work equally well in this recipe. The seasoning is mild to let the meat's flavor star. Adjust the salt and add seasonings to your liking. It is best to make jerky without salt or other seasonings for Fort Mandan Pemmican (see page 81).

2 pounds buffalo, elk, or venison roast or steak	1/2 teaspoon freshly ground black pepper
1 to 1 1/2 teaspoons salt	Dash of cayenne

To make slicing easier, partially freeze the meat for 20 minutes to 1 hour. Slice the meat with the grain into strips 1/2-inch thick, 4 to 6 inches long. Trim any remaining fat. Place the meat strips, salt, pepper, and cayenne in a bag. Seal and shake the bag to coat the meat. Line two 15 x 10-inch pans with aluminum foil. Place wire baking racks in each. Arrange meat strips on racks.

Heat a charcoal grill. Let the coals burn to medium. If necessary, use bricks to set up a second level for the second pan. Pans will be 5 to 10 inches from the coals. Roast over medium to medium-low coals for 2 1/2 to 3 hours or until the meat is dry, but still slightly chewy. Add more charcoal as needed. Rearrange pans half-way through cooking. Or dry in 250°F oven (see Note) for 2 1/2 to 3 hours, or until the meat is dry, but slightly chewy.

Jerky: Buffalo, Elk, or Venison, continued

Or dry in 250°F oven (see Note) for 2 1/2 to 3 hours, or until the meat is dry but still slightly chewy. For best results, store in the refrigerator or freezer.

Makes 1/2 to 3/4 pounds jerky.

NOTE: Food safety guidelines advise that meats cooked at temperatures lower than 300°F are subject to bacterial growth during cooking. Use your own discretion when making jerky.

Twenty-First Century Buffalo

BUFFALO HERDS HAVE returned to America and Canada. Both tribal and non-tribal people raise over 300,000 buffalo in 38 states. Buffalo need extensive grass pastures for grazing. Humans usually build strong fences to protect the still wild buffalo from the twenty-first century.

Retail stores now carry buffalo roasts, steaks, and ground meat. Lewis and Clark's hunters shot elk and deer as well. The best way to get good elk or venison is to know a hunter who will share or become a hunter yourself. Both elk and buffalo are leaner than cattle and, consequently, have a thicker grain than commercially sold beef. Venison has a finer texture. The flavors of each are distinct.

23 August 1804
Clark[iii]

"I went out and Killed a fine Buck, J[oseph] Fields Killed a Buffalow, 2 Elk Swam by the boat whilst I was out and was not Killed, many guns fired at it .... Capt. Lewis went out with [12] men & brought the buffalow to the river at this bend."

69

17 September
1804

Lewis[iv]

*"[we] regailed ourselves
on half a bisquit each
and some jirk of Elk
which we had taken the
precaution to put in our
pouches in the morning
before we set out."*

Hardtack Biscuits

IN THE LEWIS and Clark lexicon, "biscuit" meant a simple, unleavened bread baked over an open fire and also called hardtack. The dry bread keeps indefinitely, especially when made without butter or other fat. Expedition members often sopped up gravy and pan juices with a torn piece of biscuit.

2 cups whole wheat flour
2 cups all-purpose flour

1/2 to 1 teaspoon salt

Combine the flours and salt in a medium bowl. Slowly stir in 1 1/2 cups of water. Knead the dough in the bowl for about 5 minutes, or until smooth. Let the dough rest for about 10 minutes.

Form dough into a 15 x 9-inch rectangle about 1/2-inch thick on a greased baking sheet. Score at 3-inch intervals. Prick liberally with the tines of a fork. Bake at 325°F for about 50 minutes, or until lightly browned. Serve immediately or cool and store in an airtight container in the refrigerator.

Makes 15 biscuits.

Prairie Plum Tart

THE TRAVELERS HAD been picking wild fruit since late May, but this is the first mention of making pastry. Clark compared the buffalo berry to plums he knew from the East: the privet (*Ligustrum vulgare*) and the damson (*Prunus domestica insititia*).

	FILLING
1 cup all-purpose flour	
1/4 cup whole wheat flour	1 1/2 to 2 pounds ripe fresh plums, pitted and sliced (see Note)
1/2 teaspoon salt	
1/4 cup lard or vegetable shortening	1/3 cup unbleached all-purpose flour
4 tablespoons butter	1/3 to 1/2 cup sugar
2 to 3 tablespoons cold water	

To make the pastry, combine the flours and salt in a medium mixing bowl. Cut in the lard and 3 tablespoons of butter with 2 knives or with a pastry blender until the mixture is the size of shelled peas. Add the water, 1 tablespoon at a time, and stir until the pastry holds together. Chill about 20 minutes. Roll out the pastry to a 10-inch circle on a lightly floured surface. Carefully transfer the pastry circle to an ungreased baking sheet.

To make the filling, toss the plums gently with the flour and sugar in a large bowl. Arrange the plums over the pastry, leaving 1 inch of pastry around the edge. Fold the pastry edge over plums. Dot the plums with 1 tablespoon of butter.

Bake in a 375°F oven for 40 to 45 minutes, or until the plums are tender. Cool for at least 15 minutes before serving.

Makes 6 to 8 servings.

NOTE: Very ripe plums will be sweeter and juicier and will make the texture of the tart softer.

24 August 1804

Clark[v]

"Great quantities of a kind of berry resembling a Current except double the Sise and Grows on a bush like a Privey, and the Size of a Damsen deliciously flavoured & makes delitefull Tarts, this froot is now ripe."

71

Three Golden Squash and Corn

WOMEN OF THE Arikara, Mandan, and Hidatsa tribes had long since mastered how to raise squash, corn, beans, and sunflowers in their river bottom gardens. Most years they supplied more than enough corn for their own villages and a surplus to trade with other tribes.

3 pounds winter squash, such as butternut, buttercup, or Hubbard (see Note)	2 cups whole kernel corn, fresh, frozen, or canned
	1/2 teaspoon salt
1 tablespoon vegetable oil or your fat of choice	1/2 teaspoon freshly ground black pepper

Peel the squash. Remove the seeds and cut the squash into 1-inch cubes. Heat the oil in a 3-quart saucepan over medium-high heat. Stir in the squash and 1 cup of water. Bring to a boil. Reduce the heat to medium-low, cover, and cook for 15 to 20 minutes, or until the squash is tender but not mushy. Stir in the corn, salt, and pepper. Cook for another 5 minutes. Serve immediately.

Makes about 5 cups.

NOTE: If desired, rinse the seeds well and remove the fibers. Soak in lightly salted water for 5 to 10 minutes. Drain and place on a baking sheet. Bake at 300°F for about 20 minutes, or until golden brown, stirring often. Eat as a snack.

Corn with Sunflower and Black Beans

EXPEDITION MEMBERS CARRIED one thousand pounds of hominy—lye-soaked, dried corn—in their initial provisions. During the winter of 1804 to 1805, they traded for more hominy, as well as parched corn, sunflower seeds, and squash raised by the Mandan and the Hidatsa women, who were expert gardeners.

1 tablespoon butter or your fat of choice	Freshly ground black pepper to taste
2 cups whole kernel corn, fresh, frozen, or canned	1/2 cup shelled sunflower seeds (see Note)
1 cup cooked black beans, rinsed and drained	Salt (optional)

Heat the butter in a large skillet. Stir in the corn, beans, and 1/4 cup of water. Add pepper. Cover and cook about 10 minutes. Stir in the sunflower seeds and add salt if desired. Serve immediately.

Makes 6 to 7 servings.

NOTE: If using unsalted seeds, add salt to taste.

11 October 1804

Clark[viii]

"Those people gave us to eate bread made of Corn & Beens, also Corn & Beans boild. a large Been [of] which they rob the mice of the Prarie which is rich & verry nurrishing also [s]quashes &c."

Here, Clark probably describes the industrious bean mouse or vole, who stockpiled the hogpeanut (*Amphicarpaea bracteata*) in quantities of up to one pint in a single place. When women of Great Plains and prairie tribes collected the hogpeanut, they usually left dried corn or other food in exchange.

MIDDLE MISSOURI
21 AUGUST TO 25 OCTOBER 1804

20 October 1804

Ordway[ix]

"... we found a large quantity of Graze the Buff. or Rabit Berryes of which we eat freely off. they are a Small red berry, Sower & Good to the taste. we have Seen them pleanty in this Country."

Berry Pudding

TRADITIONALLY, PEOPLE PUMMELED berries with stones and formed the mass of berries into patties. The patties cooked with water made berry sauce. Many Great Plains Lakota and Dakota cooks still make Berry Pudding, usually with the modern addition of sugar to sweeten and flour to thicken. Thanks to Ike Swan for this version.

6 cups Juneberries (also called serviceberries), buffalo berries, choke-cherries (*Prunus virginiana*), or blueberries (*Vaccinium sp.*), fresh or frozen

1 cup sugar
1/2 cup all-purpose flour

Combine the berries, sugar, and 1 cup of water in a saucepan. Bring to a boil. Reduce the heat to medium-low and cook the berries for 5 minutes.

Beat together the flour and 3/4 cup water until the mixture is smooth. Beat 1/2 cup hot berry liquid into the flour mixture, then stir all at once into the berry mixture. Return the mixture to a boil, stirring constantly, for 2 to 3 minutes, or until the mixture is thickened and glossy.

Makes 3 1/2 to 4 cups pudding.

Notes

[i] Meriwether Lewis and William Clark, *The Journals of the Lewis and Clark Expedition*, 13 volumes, ed. Gary E. Moulton (Lincoln, Nebraska: University of Nebraska Press, 1983 – 2001). Lewis, 3:66.

[ii] Ibid., Clark, 3:119.

[iii] Ibid., 2:502.

[iv] Ibid., Lewis, 3:81.

[v] Ibid., Clark, 2:505.

[vi] Ibid., 3:147.

[vii] Ibid., 3:162-63.

[viii] Ibid., 3:159.

[ix] Ibid., Ordway, 9:89.

1 November 1804

Clark recorded these words by the Mandan chief Sheheke-shote,[i]

"...if we eat you Shall eat, if we Starve you must Starve also, our village is too far to bring the Corn to you, but we hope you will Call on us as you pass to the place you intend to Stop"

CHAPTER SIX

Great Plains Winter Camp
26 October 1804 to 7 April 1805

Sacagawea, Charbonneau, and Jean Baptiste Join the Expedition

THE LEWIS AND Clark Expedition arrived in the Mandan and the Hidatsa homelands in late October. The captains assumed they would establish good relations while they made winter camp and secure plenty of supplies from trading and hunting. Indeed, Sheheke-shote, a Mandan chief, offered a peace pipe and welcomed the visitors.

Hidatsa leaders expressed reservations about the Corps' purposes but did not block the Corps' plan to build a fort. Neither captain commented directly on reasons for calling it Fort Mandan with no mention of the Hidatsa.

The Corps hunted and socialized throughout the winter with the Mandans. However, the Hidatsa left their mark on Thomas Jefferson's venture when Sacagawea or Sakakawea (the Hidatsa spelling), a young Shoshone who lived among the Hidatsa, and her husband, the French-Canadian Toussaint Charbonneau, agreed to join the travelers (see page 90).

A Trading Center

LOCATION AND THE golden wealth of the Hidatsa and Mandan gardens made their villages an international trading center. Lewis and Clark joined a long line of visitors, including tribes from all directions as well as French trappers and English agents for the British fur companies.

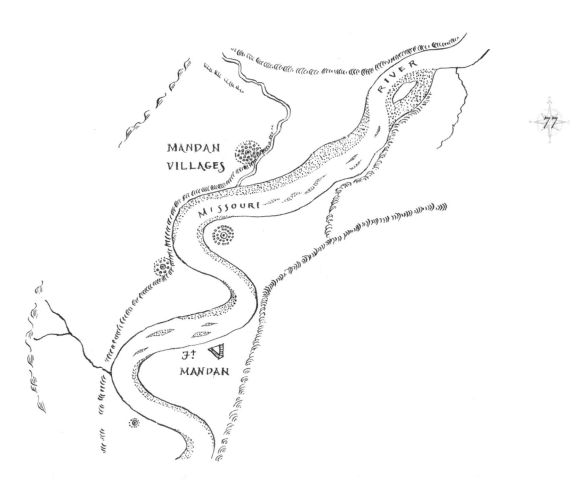

MANDAN VILLAGES

RIVER

MISSOURI

Ft MANDAN

GREAT PLAINS WINTER CAMP
26 OCTOBER 1804 TO 7 APRIL 1805

As Told by Buffalo Bird Woman

TRIBAL FOOD TRADITIONS and their rituals have for centuries been passed on by stories and example. From one generation to the next, the practice and the information are almost inseparable. The oral tradition vests the power in the person practicing the tradition, the person who gives it to the next generation.

In 1906 Buffalo Bird Woman, her son Edward Goodbird, and her brother Wolf Chief met a Presbyterian minister, Gilbert Wilson. Over the next eleven years, Wilson recorded Buffalo Bird Woman's words, as translated by her son. She described how she, a Hidatsa and a woman, practiced agriculture.

Buffalo Bird Woman's descriptions suggest deep understanding of every aspect of the seasons of agriculture. She tells about each crop and its varieties and how to grow and harvest it best. She speaks of five different kinds of corn and three kinds of beans. Bird Woman liked black beans the best. By the early twentieth century, she and other Hidatsa found that white traders preferred white beans. She says that squash more than three and one-fourth inches around and four days old is not fit to eat. She explains how she and her father preserved squash blossoms by the basketful. She details what frost does to sunflowers and how to store dried produce for the winter.

Wilson considered himself a scribe only. In 1917 the Minnesota Historical Society published *Agriculture of the Hidatsa Indian: An Indian Interpretation*. Under the title *Buffalo Bird Woman's Garden*[ii], the book was republished in 1987, and it continues to be in print.

Buffalo Bird Woman's life and work in the early 1900s probably was little changed from that of her grandparents in the early 1800s, the time of the Lewis and Clark Expedition's Fort Mandan stay. Her descriptions have contributed to choices of ingredients and recipes in this book.

Buffalo Bird Woman's story reveals some of the knowledge and a hint of the practices of her world not only to her descendants but to all who live with the challenges of modern life.

Hominy and Sunflower Cakes

28 October 1804

Clark[iii]

*"we had Several presents
from the Woman of Corn
boild homney, Soft Corn
&c. &c."*

BUFFALO BIRD WOMAN preferred ashes from ash and elm trees when preparing hominy. Powdered lime is a substitute (see page 45).

Cooks for the Corps probably used lard in a recipe like this. Butter may suit your taste better.

I can (14 1/2 ounces) white hominy (about 1 1/2 cups)	3 tablespoons lard or butter
I can (14 1/2 ounces) yellow hominy (about 1 1/2 cups)	4 to 5 tablespoons water
1/4 cup shelled sunflower seeds (see Note)	2 tablespoons vegetable oil, for frying
Salt (optional)	Warm syrup, honey, or berry jam, for serving

Rinse the hominy thoroughly. Drain well. Transfer to the bowl of a food processor and process until coarsely ground, about 10 bursts. Add the sunflower seeds and process for about 5 bursts.

Add the lard and 3 tablespoons water. Process once or twice. Add more water, as needed, and process to make the mixture hold together, 2 to 4 bursts. Form into patties, 3 1/2-inches round and 1/4-inch thick.

Heat 2 teaspoons of the oil in a large skillet over medium heat. Cook the patties, 3 to 5 minutes on each side. Remove the cooked patties to a platter and cook the remaining patties in remaining oil. Serve as a main dish or side dish. Good with warm syrup, honey, or berry jam.

Makes 8 to 10 cakes.

NOTE: If using unsalted seeds, add salt to taste.

79

19 November
1804

32 deer, 12 elk,
and 1 buffalo

7 December
1804

11 buffalo

8 December
1804

8 buffalo and 1 deer

10 December
1804

9 buffalo

12 February
1805

40 deer, 3 buffalo,
and 16 elk

Roasted Buffalo with Sage

WINTER TEMPERATURES DROPPED to -40°F, and blizzards left grazing lands covered with snow. Animals tended to be thin. The men hunted often, according to the Journals, including the days listed to the left.

One 3-pound buffalo roast

1/4 to 1/3 cup stone-ground cornmeal

1/4 teaspoon freshly ground pepper

1 to 2 tablespoons vegetable oil or other fat

1 tablespoon fresh sage leaves

Combine the buffalo, cornmeal, and pepper. Heat 1 tablespoon of the oil in a heavy roasting pan. Add the roast and brown on every side, about 5 to 7 minutes, adding the remaining tablespoon oil, if needed. Pour in 2 cups of water. Arrange the sage leaves on top of the roast. Cover, turn the heat to medium-low, and simmer the roast for about 2 hours. Let stand about 10 minutes. Carve and serve.

Makes 6 to 8 servings.

Fort Mandan Pemmican

MARILYN HUDSON, Louise Holding Eagle, and Delores Sand, who are all elders and enrolled members of the Three Affiliated Tribes—Mandan, Hidatsa, and Arikara—in North Dakota, guided this recipe and the Fort Mandan Corn Balls (see page 84) through development. They prefer pemmican without added fat while other traditions may call for added suet or lard, which makes the pemmican stick together.

Pemmican dates back to the earliest hunters. Traditional recipes vary from tribe to tribe. The word is said to come from the Abnaki *pemikan,* and the Cree *pimikan.* Pemmican is a good source of protein and vitamin C.

1/4 pound unsalted buffalo jerky (see page 68)	2 tablespoons Juneberries (also called serviceberries), buffalo berries, or blueberries, fresh, frozen, or canned

Cut the jerky into 1-inch pieces. Place in the bowl of a food processor and process until the jerky is shredded into tiny pieces. Put jerky in bowl. If any large pieces are left, remove them. Place fruit in the food processor bowl and process until fruit is finely ground. Stir fruit into jerky until the mixture is fluffy, like the texture of loose tobacco. Store in the refrigerator in a sealed bag or jar. Eat out of hand, a teaspoon or so at a time.

Makes 3/4 cup pemmican.

6 February 1805

Lewis'

"the blacksmiths take
a considerable quantity
of corn today in payment
for their labour. the
blacksmith's have proved
a happy resoce to us in
our present situation as
I believe it would have
been difficult to have
devised any other method
to have procured corn
from the natives."

Parched Sweet Corn

THE FORT MANDAN command learned quickly that they did not have enough beads, corn mills, and other small items to trade for the bushels of corn they needed during and after the winter of 1804 to 1805. The blacksmiths helped solve this problem.

Many corn-growing tribes called the season's first tender corn, what we refer to as sweet corn, green corn. Tribal women had dozens of ways to cook and preserve corn. Parched or roasted green corn, especially grilled, adds a fresh dimension to soups and stews.

4 large ears sweet corn or 4 cups frozen, whole kernel corn, defrosted	2 teaspoons oil or fat of your choice Salt

For the fresh corn, cut the kernels from the cob. Place the fresh or frozen corn in a large strainer and dip it directly in boiling water for about 30 seconds. Drain the corn.

Spread corn kernels on a large baking sheet. Drizzle with the oil and toss well. Place on a grill over low coals or in a heavy skillet over medium to medium-low heat. Roast, stirring often, for 20 to 30 minutes, or until the kernels are golden brown.

Serve as a side dish or add to other dishes calling for whole kernel corn (see pages 72, 73, 85, 86, and 93).

Makes about 2 cups.

Parched Dried Corn

CORN HAS TO be dried after the full range of starch has developed in the kernels. Sweet corn shrinks and turns pale as it dries. Mature corn hardens as moisture evaporates; it does not shrivel, and it retains its deep color.

1 cup dried corn kernels

Rinse corn in cool water. Place kernels on baking sheet and bake in a 275°F oven for about 2 hours, stirring occasionally. Turn off oven and leave pan in oven for another hour. Use for Fort Mandan Corn Balls (see page 84).

To grill: Place the corn on a baking sheet. Roast over low coals for 10 to 20 minutes, or until the kernels pop and turn golden brown. Stir often and watch carefully.

To prepare on stovetop: Heat 1 teaspoon oil in a heavy 9-inch skillet. Stir in the corn and cook over medium-low heat for 7 to 10 minutes, or until the kernels pop and turn golden brown. Stir often and watch carefully.

Makes 1 cup parched corn.

19 February 1805

Clark[vi]

"our Smiths are much engaged mending and makeing Axes for the Indians for which we get Corn."

83

30 December
1804

Ordway[vii]

"a great nomber of the
Mandans came to Trade
with us. they Brought us
corn & Beans Squasshes,
also a Some of their kind
of Bread which they
make of pearched corn
and beans mixed to gether
& made in round balls.
they have a Sweet kind
of corn which they Boil
considerable of it when it
is in the milk & drys it
which they keep through
the winter Season."

Fort Mandan Corn Balls

BUFFALO BIRD WOMAN says Gummy Corn, a sticky variety, is best for corn balls. Few gardeners, tribal or not, offer this traditional variety for sale. Seeds, however, are available (see page 156).

Parched Dried Corn (page 83) gives Corn Balls the best flavor and texture. This is a Corn Ball as the Expedition may have made it with advice from their hosts. Thanks to Marilyn Hudson, Louise Holding Eagle, and Delores Sand for their guidance.

2 cups Parched Dried
Corn (page 83)

2 teaspoons sugar
or to taste

1/4 cup ground
Juneberries, buffalo
berries, or blueberries,
fresh, or canned, drained

1/2 cup melted suet
or lard (see Note)

Grind the corn in a grinder or food processor. (Traditionally, women ground corn with ever-smoother large stones.) Sift the cornmeal to remove larger pieces that resist grinding. Makes about 1 1/2 cups sifted meal.

Mix the meal with the sugar. Stir in the berries to mix completely. Drizzle the melted suet over the mixture and stir until the mixture holds together. Form into 1 1/4-inch balls. Enjoy in small bites for snacks.

Makes about 16 corn balls.

NOTE: Lard also works in this recipe, but the balls will not hold together if butter or vegetable oil is used.

Garden Bounty with Salted Meat

PACKAGED DRIED BEEF is a modern substitute for dried buffalo. If you prefer a vegetarian main dish, leave out the meat and meat broth and substitute vegetable broth.

I small winter squash, such as butternut, buttercup, or hubbard (about 1 1/2 pounds), seeded and peeled

I cup beef broth or Portable Soup (page 18) to taste plus I cup water

I package (2 1/2 ounces) dried beef, thinly sliced

3 cups Parched Sweet Corn (page 82)

I cup cooked red or black beans

1/2 cup dried blueberries or mixed dried berries

Salt (optional)

Pepper (to taste)

1/2 cup salted sunflower seeds, chopped, (see Note)

Cut the squash into I-inch cubes. Combine the squash, broth, and dried beef in a medium saucepan. Heat to a boil. Reduce the heat and simmer for about 15 minutes, or until squash is tender. Stir in the corn, beans, berries, salt and pepper to taste. Cover and cook for 10 to 15 minutes more. To serve spoon into a serving dish and sprinkle with sunflower seeds.

Makes 6 main-dish servings or 12 side-dish servings.

NOTE: If using unsalted seeds, add salt to taste.

20 December 1804

Clark[viii]

"[Little Crow's wife] made a Kettle of boild Simnins [squash], beens, Corn & Choke Cherris with the Stones which was paletable This Dish is Considered, as a treat...."

85

GREAT PLAINS WINTER CAMP
26 OCTOBER 1804 TO 7 APRIL 1805

25 December
1804

Ordway[ix]

"our officers Gave the party a drink of Taffee [a kind of rum].
we had the Best to eat that could be had, &
continued firing dancing & frolicking dureing the whole day....
we enjoyed a merry cristmas...."

86

Corn and Dried Meat Soup

ON A COLD prairie evening the sun sets by 4:30 p.m. The Lewis and Clark Expedition had most of the ingredients necessary for a hot winter soup. Green onions for color are a modern addition.

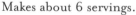

2 teaspoons vegetable oil	1 teaspoon sugar
5 green onions, chopped (about 1/2 cup)	1/2 to 1 teaspoon salt
1 1/2 cups Parched Sweet Corn (page 82)	1/2 teaspoon freshly ground black pepper
1 package (2 1/2 ounces) dried beef, thinly sliced	1/4 teaspoon crushed red pepper

Heat the oil in a medium saucepan and sauté the onions just until limp. Add the corn and sauté for about 2 minutes. Stir in the beef, sugar, salt, pepper, and crushed red pepper. Add 3 cups of water. Bring to a boil. Reduce the heat and simmer for about 30 minutes. Serve immediately.

Makes about 6 servings.

Stewed Plums and Berries

SACAGAWEA DELIVERED HER first child, a son, Jean Baptiste, on 11 February 1805. She is said to have been brought to the Missouri River after a skirmish between the Shoshone and the Hidatsa. She may have been as young as fourteen and as old as seventeen when she, her husband, and their almost two-month-old son left Fort Mandan with the Expedition.

Plums, Juneberries, chokecherries, buffalo berries, gooseberries (*Ribes v.*), and currants (*Ribes v.*) grow throughout the Great Plains and especially thrive in wet years. Use any combination for this fruit-sweetened dish.

1 1/2 pounds plums, pitted	2 cups Juneberries (also called serviceberries), chokecherries, buffalo berries, or blueberries, fresh or frozen

Combine the plums, berries, and 1/4 cup of water in a medium saucepan. Bring to a boil over medium-high heat. Reduce the heat to medium-low and cook for about 30 minutes. Cool and serve.

Refrigerate for 2 to 3 days or freeze in a sealed container for up to 2 months.

Makes about 8 to 10 servings.

20 January 1805

Clark[x]

"one of the [wives] of Shabownes...being Sick, I ordered my Servent to, give her Some froot Stewed and tee at dift Tims..."

87

Spring Thaw

DURING THE LENGTHENING days of mid-March 1805, Clark had his command making all preparations for the trip west in the red and the white pirogues, and six newly made canoes, as well as for the keelboat's return journey to St. Louis. On 15 March 1805, Clark wrote, **"a fine day I put out all the goods & Parch meal Clothing &c to Sun, a number of Indians here to day. They make maney remarks respecting our goods &c. Set Some men about Hulling Corn &c."**[xi]

Members of the Expedition and their hosts had moved easily during the winter from one side of the frozen Missouri to the other. Warmer days started the spring thaw causing the river to crumble into ice floes before melting. Geese and ducks squawked overhead on their spring migration. Clark recorded a buoyant atmosphere on 31 March 1805: **"all the party in high Spirits they pass but fiew nights without amuseing themselves danceing possessing perfect harmony and good understand towards each other."**[xii]

The Expedition finished packing the pirogues on 6 April 1805, ready for departure the next day.

[i] *William Clark Papers,* Box 11, Folder 13 Clark Family Collection Missouri Historical Society.

[ii] Gilbert Wilson, *Buffalo Bird Woman's Garden* (St. Paul: Minnesota Historical Society Press, 1987 – ca. 1917).

[iii] Meriwether Lewis and William Clark, *The Journals of the Lewis and Clark Expedition,* 13 volumes, ed. Gary E. Moulton (Lincoln, Nebraska: University of Nebraska Press, 1983–2001). Clark, 3:208.

[iv] Ibid., 3:297.

[v] Ibid., Lewis, 3:288.

[vi] Ibid., Clark, 3:298.

[vii] Ibid., Ordway, 9:106.

[viii] Ibid., Clark, 3:261.

[ix] Ibid., Ordway, 9:106.

[x] Ibid., Clark, 3:277.

[xi] Ibid., 3:313.

[xii] Ibid., 3:322, 324.

Notes

_____

_____

_____

_____

_____

_____

_____

_____

_____

_____

_____

_____

_____

_____

_____

_____

_____

_____

GREAT PLAINS WINTER CAMP
26 OCTOBER 1804 TO 7 APRIL 1805

13 June 1805

Lewis'

"my fare is really sumptuous this evening; buffaloe's humps, tongues and marrowbones, fine trout parched meal pepper and salt, and a good appetite; the last is not considered the least of the luxuries."

CHAPTER SEVEN

The Upper Missouri and the Great Falls 8 April to 27 July 1805

Another Beginning

EXTRAORDINARY LUCK OFTEN laid itself in the path of Meriwether Lewis and William Clark. The unexpected addition of a family unit to the thirty-one-member command was one of those strokes of good fortune.

The Hidatsa had warned the captains they would need horses to cross the mountains that blocked an all-water route to the Pacific Ocean. Sacagawea spoke Shoshone, her first language and that of the tribe with whom the Expedition needed to trade for horses. When she left Fort Mandan with her husband, Toussaint Charbonneau, and their son, Sacagawea had the role of translator. The captains seemed to set aside whatever reservations they may have had about a woman and a baby being on the trip. They needed Sacagawea.

Within two days, she was digging roots to vary the Expedition's diet. When her pirogue got caught up in white water, Sacagawea saved provisions, journals, and tools, all while holding her baby. Charbonneau is most lauded in the journals for making Buffalo *Boudin Blanc* (see page 96) for the group.

More Meat

The travelers again reveled in the abundance of game to satisfy their hunger for meat. They shot and cooked not only buffalo but beaver and bear. An old bear supplied several gallons of oil from his winter fat stores. Lewis noted that beaver was **"a most delicious morsel."** A single roasted beaver made a meal for two men.

Luxury

While the Corps did not dwell upon their comforts, neither did they reject moments of gustatory satisfaction. Clark wrote on 25 June 1805 that he drank coffee, **"a rarity,"** for the first time since Fort Mandan.

9 April 1805

Lewis[ii]

"when we halted for dinner [Sacagawea] busied herself in serching for the wild artichokes which the mice collect and deposit in large hoards. this operation she performed by penetrating the earth with a sharp stick about some small collections of drift wood. her labour soon proved successful, and she procurrd a good quantity of these roots."

Roasted Jerusalem Artichokes

A SUNFLOWER FAMILY member, Jerusalem artichoke (*Helianthus tuberosus*) still grows easily in the Great Plains. In supermarkets, the root is featured as a specialty vegetable, sometimes called sunchoke.

8 to 10 Jerusalem artichokes (about 1 pound)

1 tablespoon suet, lard, or butter

1/3 cup shelled sunflower seeds

Salt (optional)

1/4 teaspoon freshly ground black pepper

Scrub the Jerusalem artichokes and thinly peel. Slice in half and arrange on a 12-inch square of aluminum foil. Dot with suet and sprinkle with sunflower seeds, salt, and pepper. Bring opposite sides of the foil together and seal the seam. Fold in the ends. Grill over medium coals or bake in 400°F oven for about 50 minutes, or until tender.

Makes 3 to 4 servings.

NOTE: If using unsalted seeds, add salt to taste.

Parched Sweet Corn and Turnip Soup

THE EXPEDITION MAY not have dug the prairie turnip if Sacagawea had not been there. Surely, her knowledge of both Shoshone and Hidatsa cooking methods added variety to their largely meat diet.

The common turnip is substituted here for prairie turnips. You will not find prairie turnips commercially and may not be welcome to dig them on tribal or Federal land.

1 tablespoon butter or other fat

1/2 large turnip, peeled and cut into 1/2-inch pieces

3 cups Parched Sweet Corn (see page 82)

2 vegetable bouillon cubes or Portable Soup (see page 18) to taste

1/2 teaspoon salt

1/4 teaspoon freshly ground pepper

3 to 4 green onions with 3 inches of greens, cut on the diagonal

Heat the butter in a large saucepan. Add the turnip and cook for 3 to 5 minutes, or until just beginning to brown. Stir in the corn, 3 cups of water, the bouillon cubes, salt, and pepper. Bring to a boil. Reduce the heat to a simmer and cook for about 20 minutes, or until the turnips are tender. Sprinkle with the green onions and serve.

Makes 4 to 6 servings.

8 May 1805
Clark[iii]

"In walking on Shore with the Interpreter & his wife…Geathered on the Sides of the hills wild Lickerish, & the white apple… and gave me to eat, the Indians of the Missouri make great use of the white apple dressed in different ways."

Buffalo, Turnip, and Berry Ragout

LEWIS'S MENTION OF ragouts and truffles morella reminds us that thoughts of home and familiar surroundings and food did cross the travelers' minds. Or Lewis may have wished to return with something new for President Jefferson and other epicures.

1 pound buffalo stew meat, cut into 1 1/2-inch cubes	1 to 3 tablespoons vegetable oil or other fat
1/3 cup stone-ground cornmeal	3 to 4 turnips, peeled and cut into eighths
1 to 1 1/2 teaspoons salt	1 medium onion, peeled and quartered
1/2 teaspoon freshly ground black pepper	1 cup fresh or 1/2 cup dried blueberries

Toss the buffalo cubes in a mixture of the cornmeal, salt, and pepper. Heat 1 tablespoon of the oil in a heavy 3-quart Dutch oven over medium-high heat. Add the buffalo and brown on all sides, stirring often, for 5 to 7 minutes, adding additional oil if needed. Reduce the heat to medium if the meat browns too fast. Stir in 2 cups of water, the turnips, onion, and blueberries. Bring to a boil. Reduce the heat to low. Cook, covered, for 1 to 1 1/2 hours, stirring and basting regularly. Serve immediately or cool, refrigerate overnight, and reheat to fully develop flavors.

Makes 4 to 5 servings.

Broiled Buffalo Steak

SACAGAWEA HAD BEEN severely ill for several days. This meal signaled her recovery, much to the captains' relief.

Fat makes meat tender. Because buffalo is very lean, watch the meat carefully and remove it from the heat the minute it is done to minimize the chance of being left with dry, tough meat.

2 pounds buffalo or beef steaks, about 1-inch thick	Salt and freshly ground black pepper

Heat a grill or broiler. Place the steaks on the grill or broiler pan. Cook about 5 minutes on each side for rare, 6 to 7 minutes for medium, and 8 to 10 minutes for well done. Remove from the heat. Sprinkle with salt and pepper to taste. Serve immediately.

Makes 6 to 8 servings.

17 June 1805

Lewis [vi]

"[Sacagawea] eats as heartily as I am willing to permit her of broiled buffaloe well seasoned with pepper and salt and rich soope of the same meat...."

95

9 May 1805

Lewis[viii]

*"it is then baptised in
the missouri with two
dips and a flirt, and
bobbed into the kettle;
from whence after it be
well boiled it is taken
and fryed with bears oil
untill it becomes brown,
when it is ready to
esswage the pangs of
a keen appetite or
such as travelers in the
wilderness are seldom
at a loss for."*

3 July 1805

Lewis[ix]

*"the Indians have
informed us that we
should shortly leave the
buffaloe country after
passing the falls; this I
much regret for I know
when we leave the
buffaloe that we shal
sometimes be under
the necessity of fasting
occasionally. and at all
events the white puddings
will be irretreivably lost
and Sharbono out of
imployment."*

Buffalo Boudin Blanc

CHARBONNEAU SHOWED OFF his cooking skills and French heritage when he prepared the mild sausage *Boudin Blanc*. This is one of only a few times the journals detail how a dish was prepared. It is one of the few recipes Lewis raved about: **"this white pudding we all esteem one of the greatest delacies of the forrest,"** (9 May 1805, Lewis.[vii])

First, Charbonneau cleaned six feet of buffalo intestine. He chopped meat from the shoulder and loin as finely as knives and technique allowed and mixed it with the best quality fat from next to the buffalo kidney and flour, salt, and pepper. Next Charbonneau, whom Lewis calls **"our skilfull opporater,"** stuffed the meat into the intestine, termed by Lewis **"the recepticle,"** and tied the ends.

This adapted, mild-flavored recipe calls for ground beef to balance the very lean ground buffalo.

3/4 cup hot water

3/4 cup cracked wheat (see Note)

I pound ground buffalo (90% lean)

I pound ground beef (85% lean)

8 green onions, finely chopped (about I cup)

2 to 3 teaspoons finely chopped fresh sage, or I teaspoon dried rubbed sage

Salt

I teaspoon freshly ground black pepper

Casings (see Mail-Order Sources, page 155)

I to 2 teaspoons vegetable oil or other fat

Pour the hot water over the cracked wheat in a small bowl. Let stand, loosely covered, for about 15 minutes. Combine the buffalo, beef, onions, sage, I teaspoon of salt, and pepper in a mixer or by hand. Add the soaked wheat and combine thoroughly.

Soak the casings in cool, salted water for about 30 minutes.

Buffalo Boudin Blanc, continued

Set up a sausage stuffer according to the manufacturer's directions. Gently fill the casings, easing the meat into 1 section, twisting the casing, and repeating until all the meat is stuffed. Sausages can be frozen at this point for up to 1 month. Thaw in the refrigerator before cooking.

To cook, place the sausages in a heavy skillet. Prick lightly. Add about 1/2 cup water. Bring to a boil. Reduce the heat to medium-low and steam the sausages, uncovered, for 3 to 5 minutes, or until the water has evaporated. Add 1 to 2 teaspoons vegetable oil to the pan and pan-fry the sausages for about 15 minutes, or until lightly browned and cooked through.

Makes 10 to 12 servings.

NOTE: Or substitute 1/2 cup stone-ground cornmeal and decrease the hot water to 1/2 cup. Proceed as directed.

The Great Falls

BESIDES THE LOOMING Bitterroot Mountains, the Great Falls of the Missouri gave the Corps one of their most physically demanding challenges. For eighteen miles around five falls, the men and Sacagawea carried, pushed, and dragged provisions, their dugout canoes, and themselves up and down steep, clay hillsides carpeted with rocks and prickly pear.

From 13 June when Lewis first heard the roar of the Falls until 15 July when the command completed the portage, the captains offered the men extra drams of whiskey and as much meat as the hunters could supply.

During the same time, Lewis had some of the command assembling the iron-frame boat made in Harpers Ferry. The men sewed and stretched animal skins around the frame. They caulked the seams with beeswax. But without tar to securely seal the boat, it did not float for long. Lewis had to count this as one of the few failures of the entire journey. He directed the men to pack up the iron pieces and leave them in a cache with pork kegs, parched meal, and other supplies for their return trip.

4 July 1805
Lewis[x]

"we had a very
comfortable dinner,
of bacon, beans, suit
dumplings & buffaloe
beaf &c. in short we had
no just cause to covet the
sumptuous feasts of our
countrymen on this day."

4 July 1805
Ordway[xi]

"it being the 4th of
Independence we drank
the last of our ardent
Spirits except a little
reserved for Sickness."

Buffalo, Bacon, and Beans

THE CORPS CELEBRATED 4 July 1805 with a main dish that later, made with beef, became the backbone of the American cowboy diet.

I pound buffalo
or beef rump roast,
cut into I-inch cubes

2 tablespoons
whole wheat flour

1/4 to 1/2 teaspoon salt

1/4 teaspoon freshly
ground black pepper

1/4 pound salt pork
or thick-sliced bacon

I medium onion,
finely chopped

1 1/2 cups cooked
Great Northern beans

4 cups buffalo or beef
broth or Portable Soup
(see page 18) to taste
plus 4 cups water

Suet Dumplings (recipe
follows), for serving
(optional)

Toss buffalo cubes in a mixture of flour, salt, and pepper. Set aside. Cook the salt pork and onions in a heavy 3-quart Dutch oven over medium heat until the pork begins to brown and the onions are translucent, 5 to 8 minutes. Shake the excess flour from the buffalo and add the buffalo to the onions. Brown buffalo on all sides, stirring often, for 5 to 7 minutes, or until the meat is browned evenly. Stir in the beans and cook another 2 to 3 minutes. Stir in the broth. Bring to a boil. Reduce the heat to low. Cook, covered, about 45 minutes, stirring often. During the last 15 minutes of cooking time, add the dumplings, if desired, as directed in the dumpling recipe.

Makes about 8 to 10 servings.

Suet Dumplings

THESE DUMPLINGS ARE as hearty and filling as they sound. Simmer them with Buffalo, Bacon, and Beans (page 98) or with Provisions Pork Stew (page 54). Butter substitutes well in place of the suet.

1 1/3 cups all-purpose flour

1/2 cup whole wheat flour

1 1/2 teaspoons baking powder

1/4 to 1/2 teaspoon salt

1/3 cup melted buffalo or beef suet (see Note) or melted butter

1/2 cup beef broth or Portable Soup (see page 18) to taste with 1/2 cup water

2 eggs, beaten

Buffalo, Bacon, and Beans for serving

Mix the flours, baking powder, and salt. With a pastry blender or with 2 knives, cut the fat into the dry ingredients. Stir in the broth and eggs just until moistened. (The mixture will be lumpy and not completely moistened.)

Drop onto the boiling Buffalo, Bacon, and Beans during the last 15 minutes of cooking time. Take care to drop dumplings on pieces of meat to help hold them up. Reduce the heat to medium-low. Cook, uncovered, for about 7 minutes. Cover and cook another 7 minutes. Serve immediately with Buffalo, Bacon, and Beans.

Makes 10 dumplings.

NOTE: To melt suet, place in a saucepan over medium-low heat until the suet melts, about 10 minutes. Strain, cover, and store in the refrigerator for 3 to 5 days.

25 June 1805

Lewis[xii]

"in the evening Drewyer and Frazier arrivd with about 800 lbs. of excellent dryed meat and about 100 lbs of tallow."

26 June 1805

Lewis cooked for his crew on this evening.[xiii]

"I collected my wood and water, boiled a large quantity of excellent dryed buffaloe meat and made each man a large suet dumpling by way of a treat."

99

Sidebar

13 July 1805

Lewis[xiv]

"*meat now forms our food prinsipally as we reserve our flour parched meal and corn as much as possible for the rocky mountains which we are shortly to enter, and where from the indian account game is not very abundant.*"

27 July 1805

Lewis[xv]

"*My two principal consolations are that from our present position it is impossible that the S.W. fork can head with the water of any other river but the Columbia, and that if any Indians can subsist in the form of a nation in these mountains with the means they have of acquiring food we can also subsist.*"

Three Forks of the Missouri

ON 25 JULY 1805, Lewis and Clark led separate groups to the headwaters of the Missouri. They found three rivers converging to launch the Missouri. They dubbed the southeast river for Secretary of the Treasury Albert Gallatin, the middle fork for Secretary of State James Madison, and the southwest fork for their patron, President Thomas Jefferson. The captains determined that the Jefferson River would take them toward the mountains.

[i] Meriwether Lewis and William Clark, *The Journals of the Lewis and Clark Expedition*, 13 volumes, Edited by Gary E. Moulton, (Lincoln, Nebraska: The University of Nebraska Press 1983-2001,). Lewis, 4:287.

[ii] Ibid. 4:15.

[iii] Ibid., Clark, 4:128.

[iv] Ibid., Lewis, 4:111.

[v] Ibid., 4:126.

[vi] Ibid., 4:303.

[vii] Ibid., 4:131.

[viii] Ibid.

[ix] Ibid., 4:354.

[x] Ibid., 4:362.

[xi] Ibid., Ordway, 9:179.

[xii] Ibid., Lewis, 4:331.

[xiii] Ibid., 4:333-34.

[xiv] Ibid., 4:379.

[xv] Ibid., 4:437.

Notes

_____

_____

_____

_____

_____

_____

_____

_____

_____

_____

_____

_____

_____

_____

_____

_____

_____

_____

THE UPPER MISSOURI AND THE GREAT FALLS
8 APRIL TO 27 JULY 1805

CHAPTER EIGHT

Over the Mountains to the Columbia
28 July to 1 November 1805

The Journey Hangs in the Balance

SACAGAWEA RECOGNIZED THE Three Forks of the Missouri as the place from where she had been taken by the Hidatsa. Her memory signaled to Lewis and Clark that Shoshone bands and their horses were nearby. The Corps moved up the Jefferson River by canoe and around its rapids on foot. Splashing water damaged some food and supplies. The party sweated during hot August days and shivered through cold nights. Food supplies dwindled and hunting was scarce. Mountaintops already had a coating of snow, a constant reminder of the coming winter. Still, they didn't meet the Shoshone.

When the Jefferson tapered into a creek, Clark and a group, including York, Sacagawea, and her husband, hauled supplies overland. Meanwhile, Lewis and a scouting party continued to seek the Shoshone. Twelve August 1805 marked a milestone: Lewis and his men came to the ice-cold stream that is the Missouri's headwaters. They walked on to the creek where the Columbia River begins. He and the men ate the last of the boiled pork for supper.

The next day, Lewis and his scouts traveled into the Lemhi Valley and walked within a mile of several Shoshone. The travelers caught up with an older woman and a girl, who appeared frightened. He offered gifts and gestured for them to lead his men to the Shoshone band. After two miles, they were met with a force of sixty warriors on horseback who questioned the woman, then greeted Lewis and his men warmly. Lewis suggested that he go to the Shoshone camp and explain his purposes. Chief Cameahwait bid them to come.

Negotiations and Results

DURING DELICATE NEGOTIATIONS over the next nine days, Cameahwait and the Shoshone weighed the merits of helping the travelers, perhaps in exchange for guns and ammunition, versus leaving immediately to hunt buffalo for their winter provisions. Lewis focused on the Expedition's need for horses, without which his command faced the grim prospect of surviving the winter in the Lemhi Valley. Lewis wasn't above making threats, including suggesting that he would block all future American trade with the Shoshone if the Expedition didn't get their horses.

The captains got twenty-nine horses; they called the place Camp Fortunate. There is not a record of the outcome of Cameahwait's 1805 Shoshone buffalo hunt. Nothing in the journals indicates that Sacagawea wanted to stay with her birth tribe.

OVER THE MOUNTAINS TO THE COLUMBIA
28 JULY TO 1 NOVEMBER 1805

Lewis[1]

"I found on enquiry of McNeal that we had only about two pounds of flour remaining. this I directed him to divide into two equal parts and to cook the one half this morning in a kind of pudding with the burries as he had done yesterday and reserve the ballance for the evening. on this new fashoned pudding four of us breakfasted...."

Blackberry– Blueberry Rolled Pudding

THE SHOSHONE MADE good use of the season's choke-cherries. Women pounded them, pits and all, and set them in the sun to dry into thin cakes, much like modern fruit leather. On 2 August, Lewis had reported picking red, yellow, deep purple, and black currants as well as black gooseberries. Lewis pronounced the yellow currant and the purple serviceberry **"excellent."**

The pudding here gives a fresh twist to summer berries and to pastry.

PASTRY

1 1/2 cups all-purpose flour

1/2 cup whole wheat flour

1/2 teaspoon salt

1/2 cup butter plus 1 tablespoon

6 to 7 tablespoons cold water

FILLING

1 1/2 cups fresh or frozen blueberries

1 1/2 cups fresh or frozen blackberries or raspberries

1/2 cup (firmly packed) brown sugar

1/2 teaspoon salt

3/4 cup hot water

To prepare the pastry, mix together the flours and combine 1 3/4 cups flour and 1/2 teaspoon salt. With a pastry blender or with 2 knives, cut in 1/2 cup butter until the mixture is the size of shelled peas. Add the water, 1 tablespoon at a time, and stir until the pastry holds together. Roll out the pastry to an 12 x 8-inch rectangle.

Blackberry-Blueberry Rolled Pudding, continued

To make the filling, mix all the berries with the brown sugar, the remaining 1/4 cup of flour, and salt. Remove and reserve 1 cup of the berries.

Spoon the berries over the pastry. Dot with the remaining 1 tablespoon butter. Roll up from the long side like a jelly roll. Moisten the edge and pinch to close the seam. Carefully transfer to a well-greased 13 x 9-inch ovenproof baking dish. Place the roll at an angle in dish, if necessary.

Bake in a 450°F oven for 12 minutes. Spoon the remaining berries on either side of the roll. Pour in 3/4 cup of hot water. Reduce the heat to 350°F. Cover loosely with aluminum foil and bake for 20 minutes. Remove the foil and bake for another 40 to 45 minutes, or until the top is golden and the fruit is bubbly inside and outside of the roll. Slice and serve with warm berry sauce.

Makes 8 servings.

12 August 1805

Lewis[ii]

"on my return to my lodge an indian called me in to his bower and gave me a small morsel of the flesh of an antelope boiled, and a peice of a fresh salmon roasted; both which I eat with a very good relish. this was the first salmon I had seen and perfectly convinced me that we were on the waters of the Pacific Ocean."

Lewis's pleasing meal on 13 August belies the meager food available in the Lemhi Valley to either the Expedition or Cameahwait's people.

-106-

Roasted Salmon

AS BUFFALO IS to the Great Plains, salmon (*Oncorhynchus sp.*) is to the Northwest.

| 1 1/2 pounds salmon fillets | Roasted Sweet and New |
| Vegetable oil (optional) | Potatoes and Onions (see page 129), for serving |

Heat a grill or broiler. Place the salmon, skin side down. Brush with vegetable oil, if desired. Cook 4 to 4 1/2 minutes per 1/2-inch thickness on each side. Fish will be moist but easily flaked. Serve immediately over a bed of Roasted Sweet and New Potatoes and Onions.

Makes 4 to 6 servings.

Reunion

CLARK'S GROUP ARRIVED at the Shoshone camp on 17 August 1805. Lewis called himself **"much gratified"** to see them again.

The reunion had more significance when Sacagawea recognized her brother, Chief Cameahwait. Every communication from the chief to the captains moved from Cameahwait in Shoshone to Sacagawea who translated to Hidatsa for Charbonneau who translated into French for François LaBiche who delivered the message in English for the captains.

Jerusalem Artichoke and Squash Casserole

CAMEAHWAIT AND THE Shoshone hunted with and ate with the Expedition. Some days they ate venison or antelope. Other days they dined upon Expedition supplies of corn, beans, and squash supplemented with local wild foods.

4 strips thick-sliced bacon cut into 1-inch squares

1 pound (8 to 10) Jerusalem artichokes, peeled and quartered

3/4 pound butternut, buttercup, or Hubbard squash, peeled and cut into 1/2-inch cubes

1/2 cup vegetable broth or beef broth or Portable Soup (see page 18) to taste and 1/2 cup water

4 green onions, chopped (about 1/2 cup)

Salt and freshly ground black pepper

Cook the bacon over medium heat for 5 to 7 minutes, or until just beginning to brown. Stir in the artichokes, squash, and broth. Cook, stirring often, about 15 to 20 minutes, or until the artichokes and squash are tender but not mushy. Remove from the heat. Toss with the green onions and add salt and pepper to taste.

Makes about 6 servings.

22 August 1805

Lewis[iii]

"I gave him [Cameahwait] a few dried squashes which we had brought from the Mandans[.] he had them boiled and declared them to be the best thing he had ever tasted except sugar, a small lump of which it seems his sister Sah-cah-gar Wea had given him."

22 August 1805

Lewis[iv]

"they resemble the Jerusalem Artichoke very much in their flavor and I thought them preferable, however there is some allowance to be made for the length of time I have now been without vegitable food to which I was always much attatched. these are certainly the best root I have yet seen in uce among the Indians."

18 September 1805
Portable Soup

THE EXPEDITION LEFT on 30 August 1805 for the mountains with their Shoshone guides. After six days, they met a large Salish tribe traveling east to hunt buffalo. (The captains mistakenly named them Flatheads in their journals.) Again, fortune delivered itself to the Expedition. The Salish were not only friendly, they had excellent horses, better than those the Expedition rode. They traded eleven horses to Lewis and Clark for seven less desirable mounts.

Fresh horses helped, but every day challenged the travelers. On good days the hunters brought back beaver, deer, or geese, but once they presented only a single grouse for a day's work. Frost, rain, and hail gave way to snow as the group hacked their way through fallen trees and along a high ridge. It had snowed all day 16 September. The men melted the snow for cooking and valued their supply of Portable Soup, now over two years old. Scholars disagree as to whether the Corps ate the candles, but they may well have. The candles were made of beef tallow or suet, familiar to their diets.

3 to 4 ounces Portable Soup (see page 18)

1 small potato, peeled and chopped

1 small onion, peeled and chopped

1 small carrot, peeled and chopped

1/2 cup chopped cooked beef (optional)

Salt and freshly ground black pepper

Combine the Portable Soup, 2 1/2 cups of water, the potato, onion, carrot, and beef, if desired. Bring to a boil. Simmer about 20 minutes, or until the vegetables are tender. Add salt and pepper to taste. Serve immediately.

Makes 2 to 4 servings.

Roots

THE EXPLORERS GOT beyond the most rugged of the mountains on 20 September 1805. They entered the territory of the Nez Percé and others who spoke Sahaptian-based languages including the Umatilla, Walulas, and Yakima. Lewis and Clark reported they were grateful for anything they found to eat, even when the most reliable food available, roots and the dried fish, did not agree with their digestive systems. They sought to eat meat as often as possible.

For much of the next ten months, the travelers relied on roots, especially when the hunters came back with little. They first ate the camas (*Camassia sp.*), what they called the **"quawmash"** or **"Pas-shi-co"** root, when they met the Nez Percé for whom the dried, cooked root was a staple. Clark described it as tasting something like an onion.

The several camas varieties belong to the hyacinth family and have a white bulb that ranges in size from a nutmeg pod to an egg. Clark recounted the lengthy cooking process that started with digging a three-foot-deep hole. They layered firewood and then rocks, three to four inches thick. After a hot fire heated the rocks, they packed mixed mud and grass over the rocks. Dry grass made the next layer, which held the roots. More grass made a cover and the roots were left to caramelize and dry in the slow heat.

20 September 1805

Clark[vi]

"[Nez Percé] gave us to eate roots dried roots made in bread, roots boiled, one Sammon, Berries of red haws some dried .... those roots are like onions, Sweet when Dried, and tolerably good in bread, I eate much & am Sick in the evening. those people have an emence quantities of Roots which is their Principal food."

29 October
1805

Clark[vii]

*"Those people are
friendly gave us to
eate fish Beries, nuts
bread of roots & Drid
beries and we Call this
the friendly Village...."*

Hazelnut-
Cornmeal Pancakes

IF THE IDEA of the Corps mixing a prairie grain and the hazelnut (*Corylus americana*), more common to the Northwest, seems fanciful, let it illustrate that Lewis and Clark carried their best knowledge and material goods from the East and never hesitated to add a local touch.

1/2 cup chopped hazelnuts	2 tablespoons vegetable oil or other fat
1 1/2 cups stone-ground cornmeal	Vegetable oil, for frying
1 teaspoon baking soda	Berry syrup, butter, honey, or sugar, for serving
1/2 teaspoon salt	

Place the hazelnuts on a baking sheet and place it about 4 inches from preheated oven broiler. Turn off the heat. Leave the nuts in the oven for 2 minutes, or until they have turned golden brown. Remove at once. Set aside.

Combine the cornmeal, baking soda, and salt. Stir in 1 to 1 1/2 cups of water and 2 tablespoons of oil all at once just until batter is moistened. Let stand at room temperature for about 10 minutes. Thin batter with additional water if necessary. Stir in the nuts.

Heat a heavy griddle over medium-high heat. Brush with 1 teaspoon oil. Reduce the heat to medium. Pour the batter by the tablespoon onto the hot griddle, cooking 4 to 6 pancakes at a time. Cook until bubbly and drying around the edges, 1 to 1 1/2 minutes. Turn and cook another 1 to 1 1/2 minutes, or until golden brown. Remove to a warm platter and repeat with remaining batter. Serve immediately with berry syrup, butter, honey, or sugar as desired.

Makes 2 to 2 1/2 dozen 3- to 4-inch pancakes.

NOTE: For a more tender pancake, replace 1/2 cup of the cornmeal with 1/2 cup whole wheat flour, add 1 egg, and reduce the oil to 1 tablespoon.

Baskets

WOMEN OF THE Plateau tribes in the western foothills refined the very practical task of weaving grasses, dogbane twine, and cattail into baskets to hold berries and roots, nuts, medicines, and dried salmon and into mats to make the walls of their homes. They coiled split red cedar roots into baskets tight enough to hold water. In them, they cooked fish, meat, and soups by adding hot rocks to the water.

Columbia River Basketry, Gift of the Ancestors, Gift of the Earth,[viii] by Mary Dodds Schlick, details basketry traditions in the Northwest and includes many photographs, including one of a basket carried home by the captains. That basket is in the Peabody Museum at Harvard University.

17 October 1805

Clark[ix]

"a woman handed him a basket of water and a large Salmon about half Dried, when the Stones were hot he put them into the basket of water with the fish which was Soon Sufficently boiled for use. it was then taken out put on a platter of rushes neetly made, and Set before me they boiled a Salmon for each of the men with me...."

111

[i] Lewis, Meriwether and William Clark, *The Journals of the Lewis and Clark Expedition*, 13 volumes, ed. Gary E. Moulton (Lincoln, Nebraska: University of Nebraska Press, 1983 – 2001). Lewis, 5:95.

[ii] Ibid., 5:83.

[iii] Ibid., 5:144.

[iv] Ibid., 5:143.

[v] Ibid., 5:211, 213.

[vi] Ibid., Clark, 5:219.

[vii] Ibid., 5:349.

[viii] Mary Dodds Schlick, *Columbia River Basketry, Gift of the Ancestors, Gift of the Earth* (Seattle: University of Washington Press, 1994).

[ix] *Journals*, Clark, 5:288.

CHAPTER NINE

A Season at Fort Clatsop
4 November 1805 to 22 March 1806

Wild Roots, Elk, and a Whale

"*OCIAN IN VIEW!* **O! the joy**,"[i] Clark declared on 7 November 1805. In fact, they had about thirty miles yet to go on the wide Columbia to their journey's halfway point.

Lewis and Clark did not take well to the Pacific Coast winter. They had to adapt to the almost constant rain, wet clothes and bedding, and limited time to properly dry any meat or fowl the hunters shot. When the hunters came back empty-handed, everyone ate pounded fish, roots, and berries traded from the Chinook and Clatsop.

The coastal tribes had been trading with British and American ships for at least ten years and extended little special treatment to the latest visitors. The captains learned quickly that a few blue beads or pieces of ribbon did not count for as much as they had on the plateau.

Rain fell almost daily until their 23 March departure. Clark worked on the maps. Lewis wrote some of his most detailed observations about culture, animals, and plants, although, oddly enough, he does not mention the potlatch tradition of feasting and gift giving. Both men regarded the Fort Clatsop deprivations with some stoicism and occasional impatience. Their command hunted and sewed skins into clothes and moccasins. There was a group outing to see a whale. Several of the men spent most of the winter at the salt works.

Cape Disappointment

During November 1805, the Expedition camped at and explored from several sites on the northwest peninsula at the mouth of the Columbia, near what had been named Cape Disappointment in 1788. After days and nights of relentless rain and wind, the Corps, notably York and Sacagawea, voted unanimously on 22 November 1805 to find a winter home further inland. They moved across the mouth of the Columbia and south to the new site 7 December 1805 and started building Fort Clatsop, named for their tribal hosts.

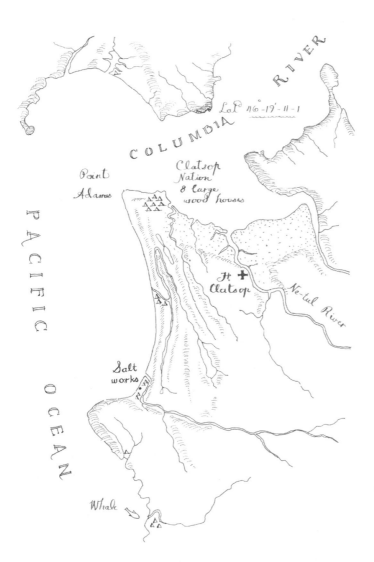

Clark settled for three hundred pounds of blubber and a few gallons of whale oil, less than he expected for the trade goods offered.

8 January 1806
Clark[iii]

"Small as this Stock is I prise it highly; and thank providence for directing the whale to us; and think him much more kind to us than he was to jonah, having Sent this monster to be Swallowed by us in Sted of Swallowing of us as jonah's did."

Lewis described eating the whale:

5 January 1806
Lewis[iv]

"it was white & not unlike the fat of Poark, tho' the texture was more spongey and somewhat coarser."

The captain's palate found whale similar in taste to beaver.

The Whale

In early January 1806, word came to Fort Clatsop that a 105-foot-long whale had washed ashore at a Kilamox village about fifteen miles away on the coast. Clark organized a party to see for themselves and add to their provisions. The captains both wrote that Sacagawea demanded to be included. Lewis wrote, **"she observed that she had traveled a long way with us to see the great waters, and that now that monstrous fish was also to be seen, she thought it very hard she could not be permitted to see either (she had never yet been to the Ocean)."**[ii]

"our party from necessaty having been obliged to subsist some lenth of time on dogs have now become extreemly fond of their flesh; it is worthy of remark that while we lived principally on the flesh of this anamal we were much more healthy strong and more fleshey than we had been since we left the Buffaloe country. for my own part I have become so perfectly reconciled to the dog that I think it an agreeable food and would prefer it vastly to lean Venison or Elk."

114

3 January 1806

Clark[vi]

"as for my own part I have not become reconsiled to the taste of this animal [dog] as yet."

More Roots

AS WOMEN ON the northern plains refined their gardening skills, women in the Pacific Northwest passed on specialized knowledge about finding and processing many varieties of edible roots. Tribal women still collect roots for food and other purposes. Outsiders may not be welcome in asking for or digging for the roots.

The recipes that follow reflect how Lewis and Clark may have prepared roots they received in trade from the Pacific Coast and Plateau Indians. Four kinds of roots receive frequent mention in the journals: Camas (see page 109), Wapato (*Sagittaria sp.*), Yampah (*Perideridia gairdneri*), and Cous (*Lomatium sp.*) None of these is available commercially.

WAPATO: Chinook women gathered wapato by the bushel from swampy areas. One method of gathering wapato was to wade among the plants and ease the tubers from the mud and water with their toes. Depending on the tribe, people ate the raw root or roasted it as Clark described on 4 November 1805. The taste has been compared to a sweet version of the common potato, such as a new potato.

YAMPAH: Clark compared yampah to fennel. Sometimes they dried yampah into cakes or mixed dried, powdered yampah with dried meat, much like Great Plains pemmican.

COUS: The captains described cous (pronounced like blouse) as tasting like sweet potato. Others say it has a hint of ginseng flavor. One of a family of roots sometimes called Indian celery, cous is ground and either formed into cakes and dried or dried and used for soups.

New Potatoes with Hazelnuts and Fennel

CHINOOK WOMEN MAY have shown Sacagawea how to find local roots. In the process of choosing the winter fort site, Clark wrote, **"[Sacagawea] in favour of a place where there is plenty of Potas."** (24 November 1805, Clark[viii]) For the next seven months, the explorers ate many pounds of roots. At times they had nothing else.

1 pound new potatoes, peeled and quartered

1 fennel bulb, peeled and quartered

1/4 cup chopped hazelnuts

1 tablespoon vegetable oil

Toss the potatoes, fennel, and hazelnuts in 12 x 9-inch baking pan. Drizzle with oil and stir to mix. Bake in a 400°F oven for 45 to 50 minutes, or until the potatoes are tender and the hazelnuts are browned.

Makes 4 to 6 servings.

4 November 1805

Clark[vii]

"[He] gave us a roundish roots about the Size of a Small Irish potato which they roasted in the embers until they became Soft, This root they call Wap-pa-to... it has an agreeable taste and answers verry well in place of bread. we purchased about 4 bushels of this root and divided it to our party."

Lewis wrote that the Indians wanted to trade only roots to the Corps, reserving the pounded fish for trade only among the Clatsops, Chinooks, and other area tribes.

24 January 1806

Lewis[ix]

"but the most valuable of all their roots is foreign to this neighbourhood I mean the Wappetoe.... this bulb forms a principal article of traffic between the inhabitants of the valley and those of this neighbourhood or sea coast."

115

Fort Clatsop Sourdough Biscuits

CLARK SEEMS TO be describing the flavor of sourdough bread in a kindness Sacagawea showed him 30 November 1805.

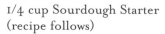

1/4 cup Sourdough Starter (recipe follows)

1/2 cup warm water or milk (120°F)

1 1/2 to 2 cups all-purpose flour

2 teaspoons brown sugar

1/2 cup whole wheat flour

1/2 teaspoon baking powder

1/4 teaspoon baking soda

1/4 teaspoon salt

1 tablespoon butter or margarine

Butter and honey, for serving

The night before or 8 hours ahead, mix the starter, water, and 1/2 cup of the all-purpose flour in a medium bowl. Cover with a clean towel. Set aside in a warm (70° to 80°F) place overnight.

The next day, stir in the brown sugar. Set aside. Combine 3/4 cup all-purpose flour, the whole wheat flour, baking powder, baking soda, and salt. Stir into the starter mixture. Beat until smooth. The mixture will be wet. Sprinkle 1 to 2 tablespoons additional flour on a clean, dry cutting board. Turn the dough onto the board. Gently form the dough into a ball. To knead the dough, push it out with the heel of your hand. Fold in the sides. Rotate a quarter turn. Repeat, adding flour by teaspoons, until a soft dough forms, about 8 turns. Take care not to add too much flour or the biscuits will be tough.

Gently press the dough into a 9 x 4-inch rectangle about 1/2 inch thick. With a 2 1/2-inch floured biscuit cutter or a 2 1/2-inch round drinking glass dipped in flour, cut into rounds. Reroll dough scraps once.

Melt the butter in a 9-inch square or round baking dish or pan. Place biscuits and trimmings in pan.

Cover with a damp towel and let rise in a warm place for 30 minutes. Bake at 375°F for 25 to 30 minutes, or until the biscuits are slightly browned and sound hollow when tapped. Remove to a wire rack. Best eaten hot. Good with butter and honey.

Makes about 8 biscuits.

Sourdough Starter

2 1/4 teaspoons
active dry yeast

2 cups warm water (120°F)

2 cups unbleached
all-purpose flour

Dissolve the yeast in the warm water. Let stand until bubbly, about 10 minutes. Stir in the flour. Cover loosely with plastic wrap. Let stand at room temperature for 24 to 48 hours, stirring occasionally.

At the end of the standing time, either use immediately as directed on page 116. Or transfer the sourdough starter to an airtight container. Refrigerate in a ceramic, glass or plastic bowl. Replenish the starter after each baking: Stir equal amounts of water and flour into starter, i.e., if you remove 1/4 cup starter, add 1/4 cup warm water and 1/4 cup flour. Let the starter stand at room temperature several hours until it bubbles. Refrigerate.

Makes 3 cups starter.

30 November 1805

Clark[x]

"[Sacagawea] gave me a piece of bread made of flour which She had reserved for her child and carefully Kept untill this time, which has unfortunately got wet, and a little Sour. this bread I eate with great Satisfaction, it being the only mouthfull I had tasted for Several months past."

5 January 1806

Lewis[xi]

"... the want of bread I consider as trivial provided, I get fat meat, for as to the species of meat I am not very particular.... and I have learned to think that if the chord be sufficiently strong, which binds the soul and boddy together, it dose not so much matter about the materials which compose it."

117

A SEASON AT FORT CLATSOP
4 NOVEMBER 1805 TO 22 MARCH 1806

Lewis[xiv]

"...they commenced the making of salt and found that they could obtain from 3 quarts to a gallon a day; they brought with them a specemine of the salt of about a gallon, we found it excellent, fine, strong, & white; this was a great treat to myself and most of the party, having not had any since the 20th ultmo.; I say most of the party, for my friend Capt. Clark declares it to be a mear matter of indifference with him whether he uses it or not; for myself I confess I felt a considerable inconvenience from the want of it..."

118

Holiday Fare

Christmas 1805

Clark[xii]

"we would have Spent this day the nativity of Christ in feasting, had we any thing either to raise our Sperits or even gratify our appetites, our Diner concisted of pore Elk, So much Spoiled that we eate it thro' mear necessity, Some Spoiled pounded fish and a fiew roots."

New Year's Day 1806

Lewis[xiii]

"our repast of this day tho' better than that of Christmass, consisted principally in the anticipation of the 1st day of January 1807, when in the bosom of our friends we hope to participate in the mirth and hilarity of the day, and when with the zest given by the recollection of the present, we shall completely, both mentally and corporally, enjoy the repast which the hand of civilization has prepared for us. at present we were content with eating our boiled Elk and wappetoe, and solacing our thirst with our only beverage *pure water*."

Salt Works

CAPTAIN CLARK DID not miss salting his food. Lewis made sure they had a steady supply at Fort Clatsop and for the return trip. At Lewis's orders, Joseph Fields, William Bratton, and Charles Gibson moved to the coast to make a camp and to boil ocean water to collect salt. During the next two months, these men scraped twenty gallons of salt in what Lewis termed, **"a very tedious operation."** The Expedition carried twelve gallons from Fort Clatsop, enough, Lewis estimated, to last until they reached their cached supplies on the Missouri.

Braised Elk Brisket

AT TIMES THE hunters walked as far as twenty miles to bring back an elk for the command. Lewis praised George Drouillard especially for his skills in the hunt.

One 2 1/2- to
3-pound elk roast

2 large onions,
peeled and cut into wedges

1/2 teaspoon
ground cinnamon

1 teaspoon salt

1/4 teaspoon freshly
ground black pepper

3 large sweet potatoes,
peeled and cut into
1 1/2-inch chunks

Place the roast in a Dutch oven. Layer the onions on top of the meat and season with cinnamon, salt, and pepper. Pour 1 cup of water over the meat and onions. Bake in a 350°F oven for 2 hours. Add the sweet potatoes and bake for 45 minutes to 1 hour longer, or until the meat and potatoes are very tender. Serve the meat and vegetables with cooking juices.

Makes 6 to 8 servings.

119

29 January 1806

Lewis[xv]

"a keen appetite supplys in a great degree the want of more luxurious sauses or dishes, and still render my ordinary meals not uninteresting to me, for I find myself sometimes enquiring of the cook whether dinner or breakfast is ready."

14 January 1806

Lewis[xvi]

"From the best estimate we were enabled to make as we dscended the Columbia we conceived that the natives inhabiting that noble stream, for some miles above the great falls to the grand rappids inclusive annually prepare about 30,000 lbs. of pounded sammon for market."

4 March 1806

Lewis[xvii]

"we live sumptuously on our wappetoe and Sturgeon."

Fort Clatsop Salmon Chowder

CHOWDER, FROM THE French *chaudière,* has its closest association with the northeastern United States. It translates well to the Pacific Coast.

4 cups vegetable or chicken broth

1/4 pound smoked salmon

1/2 pound sweet potatoes, peeled and diced

1/2 cup sliced fennel

1 small onion, peeled and chopped

Salt and freshly ground black pepper

1 tablespoon chopped fennel fronds

Fort Clatsop Sourdough Biscuits (see page 116), for serving (optional)

Bring the broth to a boil. Stir in the salmon, potatoes, fennel, and onion. Add salt and pepper to taste. Return to a boil. Cover and reduce the heat to medium-low and simmer for 20 to 25 minutes, or until the vegetables are tender. Sprinkle with chopped fennel fronds and serve immediately with Sourdough Biscuits, if desired.

Makes 6 to 7 servings.

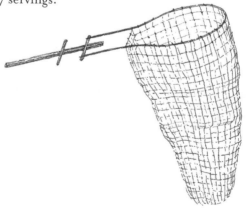

Duck Breast with Dried Fruit Sauce

LEWIS RECOGNIZED THE canvasback (*Aythya valisineria*) duck as one that lived on the Potomac and Delaware Rivers. He was the first to note for science that the canvasback, the coot (*Fulica americana*), and the blue-winged teal (*Querquedula discors*) thrived in the West as well as the eastern United States.

Berries added sweetness and color to the Corps' Fort Clatsop diet. The Corps added the salal (*Gaultheria shallon*), a black, cherry-sized berry, and the evergreen huckleberry (*Vaccinium ovatum*) to scientific knowledge.

There is no record, but the explorers could have made a meal such as this with the duck and dried berries.

3 tablespoons vegetable oil	Salt and freshly ground black pepper
6 duck breasts (about 1 1/2 pounds), fresh or frozen (if frozen, thaw before using)	1 cup dried blueberries or mixed dried berries

Heat 1 1/2 tablespoons of the oil in a skillet over medium-high heat until hot. Season the duck breasts with salt and pepper and place half of them in the pan. Fry for 4 minutes. Turn the duck, cover the skillet, and cook about 4 minutes longer, or until the duck is firm but still pink in the center. Remove to a plate and keep warm. Repeat with the remaining oil and duck breasts.

Stir 1 cup of water and the dried fruit into the juices in the skillet. Bring the mixture to a boil. Cook, stirring, for 4 to 5 minutes, or until reduced slightly. Serve the duck with the fruit and pan juices.

Makes 6 servings.

Scrambled Eggs with Smoked Salmon

NESTING DUCKS AND other fowl may have supplied eggs for the Corps.

6 eggs
1/4 pound smoked salmon
1/4 teaspoon salt

1/4 teaspoon freshly ground black pepper
1 teaspoon vegetable oil

Beat the eggs well. Break the salmon into small pieces and stir into the eggs with salt and pepper. Heat the vegetable oil in a 9-inch skillet over medium heat. Pour in the egg-salmon mixture and cook about 10 minutes, lifting the cooked eggs on the bottom to let the uncooked mixture run to bottom. Turn once.

Makes 5 to 6 servings.

HAZELNUT-POTATO SMOKED SALMON SCRAMBLED EGGS: Stir 1/2 cup cooked potatoes and 1/4 cup roasted hazelnuts into the egg and salmon mixture. Cook as above.

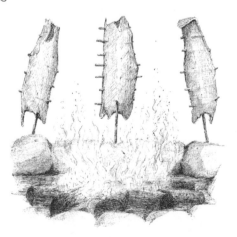

Notes

---

i Meriwether Lewis and William Clark, *The Journals of the Lewis and Clark Expedition*, 13 volumes, ed. Gary E. Moulton (Lincoln, Nebraska: University of Nebraska Press, 1983 – 2001). Clark, 6:58.

ii Ibid., Lewis, 6:168.

iii Ibid., Clark, 6:183-84.

iv Ibid., Lewis, 6:166.

v Ibid., 6:162.

vi Ibid., Clark, 6:163.

vii Ibid., 6:17.

viii Ibid., 6:84.

ix Ibid., Lewis, 6:233-34.

x Ibid., Clark, 6:97.

xi Ibid., Lewis, 6:166.

xii Ibid., Clark, 6:138.

xiii Ibid., Lewis, 6:151-52.

xiv Ibid., 6:166.

xv Ibid., 6:245.

xvi Ibid., 6:203.

xvii Ibid., 6:378.

xviii Ibid., 6:395.

xix Ibid., 6:441.

xx Ibid., 6:444.

Chapter Ten

Up the Columbia, Over Mountains, and Down the Yellowstone
23 March to 12 August 1806

The Nez Percé Help Again

THE CAPTAINS SET their departure from Fort Clatsop at the earliest possible moment. They had traded for one canoe and stole another when Chief Coboway declined their trade for it. The captains justified taking the canoe due to six elk taken from the Corps earlier in the winter. The theft was one of the few blatantly hostile acts by the Expedition toward native tribes.

Almost daily they met with tribes along the route and traded for much of their food. Very few trade goods remained beyond their kettles, the skin clothing they had made over the winter, and their personal gear. Even Meriwether Lewis's dress uniform coat had been spent in trade for one of the canoes they needed. William Clark's medical skills came to be one of the Corps' most valuable commodities that spring. He prescribed eyewashes, drained wounds, and applied salves in return for food.

They paddled up the Columbia in spring flood. The explorers had to continue to take care in their relations with the tribes, especially counting on successful negotiations with the Nez Percé for horses. The captains had to weigh every decision with their goal to reach St. Louis by the end of the season. But nothing in their control made the mountain snows melt faster.

CANADA

WASHINGTON

Fort
Clatsop

Columbia R.

Snake R.

Salmon R.

Missouri River

ROUTE OF LEWIS

MONTANA

Yellowstone River

ROUTE OF CLARK

POMPEY'S
PILLAR

BOILING
SPRINGS

OREGON

IDAHO

WYOMING

How to Cook a Bear

LEWIS FIRST WROTE about the grizzly bear (*Ursus horribilis*) on the menu in April 1805. He described the Nez Percé cooking method for bear when the hunters brought in two, a male and a female, in May 1806. The cooks made an earthen oven, first building a fire and arranging smooth river stones on top of it. They covered the stones with pine boughs, laid meat on top, then added a final layer of pine boughs and poured water over all. Finally, they packed four inches of soil over the pile and let it bake for three hours.

Lewis's opinion of roasted bear? On 14 May 1806, he wrote, **"I taisted of this [bear] meat and found it much more tender than that which we had roasted or boiled, but the strong flavor of the pine distroyed it for my pallate."**[1]

126

Braised Fennel

BRAISED FENNEL RESEMBLES cooked onions but with a subtle and slightly sweet taste.

3 medium fennel, halved, or 6 small whole fennel	1 to 2 tablespoons vegetable oil
1 cup chicken broth	2 teaspoons anchovy paste

Trim fennel stalks to the bulb and slice 1/4 inch from the bottom of the bulb. Mix the broth, oil, and anchovy paste in a medium saucepan. Add the fennel to the broth mixture. Bring to a boil. Cover and cook over medium-low heat, turning the fennel several times, for about 40 minutes, or until the fennel is tender. Serve immediately with the broth mixture in a pitcher on the side.

Makes 4 to 6 servings.

Roasted Parsnips with Pine Nuts

NATIVE TRIBES THROUGHOUT the western plateau and basin have long collected and enjoyed pine nuts for food. The variety available among the Nez Percé was *Pinus ponderosa*. Pine nuts of other varieties are found around the world.

4 parsnips, peeled and cut into 1-inch slices (see Note)

1 1/2 to 2 tablespoons vegetable oil

1/4 teaspoon salt

1/4 teaspoon freshly ground black pepper

1/2 cup pine nuts

Place the parsnips on a baking pan and brush with vegetable oil. Sprinkle with salt and pepper. Roast at 400°F for 10 minutes. Lower the heat to 350°F and stir in the pine nuts. Roast, stirring several times, about 20 minutes more, or until the parsnips and pine nuts are golden brown. Serve immediately.

Makes 6 servings.

NOTE: If parsnips are more than 1-inch in diameter, slice lengthwise in half.

8 May 1806

Lewis[iii]

"... [Pine nut is the] seed of the longleafed pine which in those moments of distress also furnishes an article of food; the seed of this speceis of pine is about the size and much the shape of the seed of the large sunflower; they are nutricious and not unpleasent when roasted or boiled."

16 May 1806

Lewis[iv]

"Sahcargarmeah geathered a quantity of the roots of a speceis of fennel [Gairdner's yampah, *Perideridia gairdneri*] which we found very agreeable food, the flavor of this root is not unlike annis seed and they dispel the wind which the roots called Cows and quawmash are apt to create particularly the latter. we also boil a small onion [Geyer's onion, *Allium geyeri*] which we find in great abundance, with other roots and find them also an antidote to the effects of the others. the mush of roots we find adds much to the comfort of our diet."

127

Lewis'

"about Noon Sergt.
Ordway Frazier and
Wizer returned
with 17 salmon and
some roots of cows....
these fish were as fat
as any I ever saw;
sufficiently so to cook
themselves without the
addition of grease;
those which were
sound were extreemly
delicious; their flesh
is of a fine rose
colour with a small
admixture of yellow."

128

Steamed Salmon

ON 19 APRIL 1806, the season's first salmon, caught in a Tenino village near the Dalles of the Columbia, signaled the beginning of the salmon run. Lewis had estimated that as many as 300,000 pounds of fish were traded among the Northwest tribes. Salmon's abundance gave the Chinook tribes a steady food supply and a reliable item to trade. Each generation passed along stories and spiritual practices related to the salmon, just as the Plains tribes revered the buffalo.

Lewis wrote about three of the five known salmon varieties (*Oncorhynchus*): the king (*O. tshawytscha*), also known as the Chinook salmon; the sockeye or blueback (*O. nerka*); and the silver or coho (*O. kisutch*). He described at different times how the fish was roasted, smoked, steamed, and boiled.

2 pounds fresh
salmon fillet

1 medium sweet onion,
peeled, halved, and thinly
sliced

1 medium fennel bulb,
peeled and thinly sliced,
fennel fronds reserved

1/2 teaspoon salt

Freshly ground black
pepper

Lay the salmon on half of a 30-inch length of heavy-duty aluminum foil. Layer the onion and fennel over the fish and season with salt and pepper. Chop the reserved fennel fronds and sprinkle 1 to 3 teaspoons over the vegetables. Fold the other half of foil over the fish and vegetables and seal the edges well. Slide the foil packet onto a baking sheet. Bake in a 425°F oven for 20 minutes. Open the packet and serve the fish hot with the vegetables.

Makes 6 to 8 servings.

Roasted Sweet and New Potatoes with Onions

THE EXPLORERS HAD abandoned their first attempt on 17 June to move through the mountains, overcome by snow still twelve to fifteen feet deep in the sunniest spots on the south hillsides. For the first time in the trip, they had to turn back. They waited until 24 June to start again with their three Nez Percé guides. The group covered as many as thirty miles a day through the mountains, still full of snow but passable. The trip took just five days compared to the seventeen long days the previous fall. Roots and some meat sustained them.

3/4 pound sweet potatoes, peeled and thinly sliced

3/4 pound new potatoes, well scrubbed and thinly sliced

1/2 pound onions, peeled and thinly sliced

4 teaspoons vegetable oil or other fat

1 to 1 1/2 teaspoons salt

Freshly ground black pepper

Toss the vegetables with the oil, salt, and pepper. Layer on 2 baking sheets. Bake at 375°F, turning the vegetables once, for 35 to 40 minutes, or until light golden brown.

Makes 4 to 6 servings.

Throughout the spring of 1806, the Expedition continued to eat camas and cous by the pound to supplement the meat brought in by hunters. Lewis lamented their continued dependence on the Nez Percé for digging the roots.

In the passage below, Lewis expresses a practical concern about being poisoned. For example, the edible camas differs from the deadly camas-like plant *Zigadenus elegans* only in the color of its spring flower. At other times of the year, the plants are identical to an untrained eye.

21 May 1806

Lewis[vi]

"we would make the men collect these roots themselves but there are several speceis of hemlock which are so much like the cows that it is difficult to discriminate them from the cows and we are affraid that they might poison themselves."

Morel Mushrooms

LEWIS'S TASTES MADE him no threat to modern mushroom collectors who gather morels (*Morchella esculenta*) as spring trees leaf out and who jealously guard their picking grounds. Special thanks to Bev Hinds for morel consultation.

2 pounds morel mushrooms

3 to 4 tablespoons butter or oil

1/4 cup all-purpose flour

Buttered toasted bread, for serving

Rinse the mushrooms thoroughly in cool water to remove sand and dirt. Pat dry on paper towels. Heat the butter in a heavy skillet. Dust the mushrooms, a few at a time, in flour and shake off the excess flour. Cook over medium-high heat for about 3 minutes, then turn. Reduce the heat to medium and cook for 5 to 7 minutes longer. Serve immediately on buttered toasted bread. Cooked mushrooms don't taste as good the second day. Go out and find some more.

Makes 4 to 6 servings.

Deep-Fried Venison

LEAN WILD GAME deep-fries beautifully. While modern cooks often leave deep-frying to restaurants, the rich flavor and fast cooking time would have appealed to the travelers.

2 pounds venison roast

Vegetable oil, for frying

Salt and freshly ground black pepper

Braised Fennel (see page 126)

Slice the venison into 1/2-inch-thick pieces, about 3 inches wide. Heat 3 inches of oil to 365°F in a heavy saucepan. Fry 2 pieces of meat at a time, about 45 seconds on each side. Drain on paper towels. Serve immediately with Braised Fennel.

Makes about 8 servings.

Boiled Meat

CLARK CONDUCTED A cooking experiment on 7 July 1806 at what he called **"Boiling Springs,"** now known as Jackson Hot Springs in Wyoming. Clark started with meat the size of his three fingers. That portion took twenty-five minutes to cook. A larger piece needed thirty-two minutes to doneness. Clark did not note the type of meat.

27 June 1806

Lewis[viii]

"our meat being exhausted we issued a pint of bears oil to a mess which with their boiled roots made an agreeable dish."

29 June 1806

Lewis[ix]

"... we fund a deer which the hunters had killed and left us. this was a fortunate supply as all our oil was now exhausted and we were reduced to our roots alone without salt."

131

Cornish Hens with Sweet Potato Stuffing

EVEN IN BUFFALO country at the height of summer, Lewis's party had to settle for pigeons instead of meat. Cornish hens, more readily available to the modern cook, make a good substitute.

2 Cornish hens (about 12 ounces each)

Salt and pepper to taste

3 medium sweet potatoes, peeled and cut into 1/2-inch cubes

1 tablespoon vegetable oil

Place the Cornish hens on a baking sheet. Sprinkle with salt and pepper inside and out. Fill the cavity loosely with sweet potatoes, letting a few sweet potatoes overflow. Brush oil on each hen. Bake in a 350°F oven for 1 1/4 to 1 1/2 hours, or until the juices run clear and the potatoes are tender. Carve the hens and serve with the sweet potatoes.

To roast on the grill: Prepare the hens on a baking sheet as above. Place to the side of hot coals. Cover the grill and roast the hens as above.

Makes 3 to 4 servings.

In the General Direction of Home

THE COMMAND CELEBRATED the mountain crossing with hot baths courtesy Lolo Hot Springs. They halted a few days at Traveler's Rest, near present-day Missoula, Montana. The captains devised a plan to make more complete explorations before directing all their energies toward home.

Lewis led a group to the north, back to the Missouri River and the Great Falls with an excursion up the Marias River where they met the Blackfoot Indians. Clark's party, including Sacagawea, traveled south to uncover a cache of food and canoes left the previous summer. They revisited the Three Forks of the Missouri and traveled more than six hundred miles up the Yellowstone River where it meets the Missouri near what is now the Montana-North Dakota border.

The command reunited on 12 August 1806, reaching the rendezvous point within days of one another.

Elk Hunting

ON 11 AUGUST 1806, Lewis spotted a herd of elk and directed Cruzatte, blind in one eye and near-sighted in the other, to join him in a hunt. Lewis shot one; Cruzatte wounded another. As Lewis loaded to fire a second shot, a bullet struck him through the left buttock and into the right. Lewis wrote, **"I instantly supposed that Cruzatte had shot me in mistake for an Elk as I was dressed in brown leather and he cannot see very well."** (11 August 1806[xi])

Lewis had it right. He spent the next week and a half draped over a canoe, recovering. However, his men ate meat on 11 August.

This is Lewis's last journal entry.

[i] Meriwether Lewis and William Clark, *The Journals of the Lewis and Clark Expedition*, 13 volumes, ed. Gary E. Moulton (Lincoln, Nebraska: University of Nebraska Press, 1983 – 2001). Lewis, 7:257.

[ii] Ibid., Clark, 7:128

[iii] Ibid., Lewis, 7:227.

[iv] Ibid., 7:264.

[v] Ibid., 7:326-27.

[vi] Ibid., 7:275.

[vii] Ibid., 8:37.

[viii] Ibid., 8:57.

[ix] Ibid., 8:61.

[x] Ibid., 8:126.

[xi] Ibid., 8:155.

Notes

CHAPTER ELEVEN

Return to St. Louis
13 August to 25 September 1806

The Long Welcome

FROM THEIR REUNION point, the captains focused on home. They pushed down the Missouri as many as sixty miles a day. In the gradual return to the familiar, the Mandans welcomed them in the midst of their summer harvest. Women served the Corps summer squash, called *simmins*. Expedition canoes couldn't hold the many bushels of corn the Mandans gave them. Clark continued to record and observe. Lewis recuperated, not taking his first steps until 22 August.

Charbonneau, Sacagawea, and Jean Baptiste left the group where they had joined it. Clark later praised Charbonneau for friendship and lauded Sacagawea, writing **"[Sacagawea] diserved a greater reward for her attention and services on that rout than we had in our power to give her at the Mandans."** (20 August 1806, Clark[i])

Clark offered to raise their son and encouraged Sacagawea to come with the boy to St. Louis. The captains invited both Mandan and Hidatsa leaders to join them for a visit to St. Louis. The Mandan Chief Sheheke-shote agreed to go and, along with an interpreter, left with the remaining Corps on 17 August 1806. The Arikara and the Yankton greeted the travelers warmly. A brief meeting with the Teton Sioux left Clark watchful, but there was not a confrontation as in 1804.

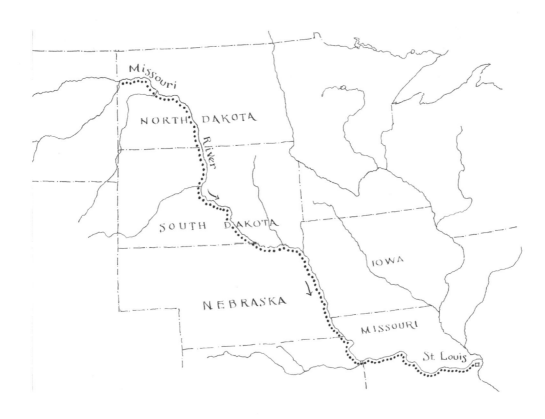

Westward Expansion Begins in Earnest

LEWIS AND CLARK witnessed the effects of their legacy during those summer days in 1806. John Colter left the Corps from the Mandan villages to travel west with two Illinois men. The Expedition traded corn with these men for hardtack, sugar, whiskey, pork, onions, flour, and tobacco. A trickle of traders and adventurers was stepping through the door swung open by the Expedition.

RETURN TO ST. LOUIS
13 AUGUST TO 25 SEPTEMBER 1806

21 August 1806
Clark[ii]

"the Mandan Chief
[Sheheke-shote] Stuck
close to me the Chief had
prepd. a Supper of
boiled young Corn,
beens & quashes of
which he gave me in
Wooden bowls."

138

Husk-Roasted Sweet Corn

MANY TRIBES CALLED the season's first corn "green corn," what we commonly call sweet corn.

| 6 ears fresh sweet corn in husk | Water |

Heat a grill. Soak the corn in water. Shake out the excess water and place on the grill. Cover and roast for 25 to 30 minutes, or until tender. Husk the corn and serve.

Makes 6 servings.

Hot Chocolate

CLARK'S CHOCOLATE HAD made a long trip from the Caribbean to soothe the captain's stomach.

1 ounce unsweetened chocolate	1/2 cup milk
2 tablespoons sugar	2 tablespoons whipping cream

Finely grate the chocolate. Mix with 1 cup water and bring to a boil. Boil to reduce by one-third. Stir in the sugar until dissolved. Pour in the milk and cream and bring to just below a boil. Serve immediately.

Makes 1 serving.

Almost Home

WILD FRUIT RIPENED along their homeward dash. The travelers picked black cherries, black currants, wild grapes, and three varieties of plums. The hunters brought in elk, buffalo, and deer, but not every day. With St. Louis just 150 miles away, the Corps took a vote: make camp and hunt for fresh meat or fill up on pawpaws (*Asimina triloba*). They chose the somewhat astringent pawpaw and pushed on.

On 18 September 1806, Clark wrote, **"we divide the buiskit which amounted to nearly one buisket per man, this in addition to the poppaws is to last is [us] down to the Settlement's which is 150 miles the party appear perfectly contented and tell us that they can live very well on the pappaws."**[iii]

12 Sept 1806

Clark[iv]

"I felt my Self very unwell and derected a little Chocolate which Mr. [Robert] McClellen gave us, prepared of which I drank about a pint and found great relief..."

17 September 1806

Clark[v]

"... [Captain John McClallen] gave us Some Buisquit, Chocolate Sugar & whiskey, for which our party were in want and for which we made a return of a barrel of corn & much obliges to him."

139

20 September
1806

Clark[viii]

"we Saw Some cows on the bank which was a joyfull Sight to the party and Caused a Shout to be raised for joy"

Later on 20 September, Clark recorded that the citizens of La Charette greeted the men with the news that the Expedition had been given up for dead.

Homecoming

AT NOON ON 23 September 1806, the canoes and pirogues reached the St. Louis river bank. Clark wrote, **"we were met by all the village and received a harty welcom from it's inhabitants &."**[vi]

The same day, Lewis wrote to President Jefferson, **"It is with pleasure that I announce to you the safe arrival of myself and party at 12 OClk. today at this place with our papers and baggage. In obedience to your orders we have penetrated the Continent of North America to the Pacific Ocean...."** (23 September 1806 , Lewis[vii])

Celebrations were in order after the 2,575-mile journey. Pierre Chouteau, the St. Louis fur trader and a friend to both Lewis and to Clark, hosted a ball on 24 September 1806. The captains received eighteen toasts. Another ball followed dinner on 25 September 1806.

Menu for a Celebration

THIS MENU REFLECTS the best meats, fruits of summer, and delicacies the frontier town had available. Recipes in bold face type appear on the following pages.

A Celebration Meal

Standing Rib Roast

Country Ham   Roast Chicken

Fresh Greens with Chive-Cream Dressing

Hot Biscuits   **Wild Grape Jelly**

Assorted Autumn Vegetables

Spicy Sweet and Sour Pickles

Nutmeg-Plum Shortcakes

Cream and Bread Pudding with Cherries

Almond Sponge Cake with Lemon Curd

Wine   Ale   Cider   Coffee

Fruits   Candies   Nuts

Standing Rib Roast

THE STANDING RIB Roast comes from the English manor tradition. In 1806 St. Louis, it was a delicacy and remains so.

Ask for a roast from the small end, the larger muscle and more tender meat. And ask to have the chine bone removed for easier carving.

One 6- to 8-pound standing rib roast (2 to 4 ribs)

Place the meat in a large baking pan and roast in a 500°F oven for 5 minutes. Lower the heat to 350°F. Roast to desired doneness.

For medium-rare, roast for 2 1/4 to 2 1/2 hours, or to an internal temperature of 135°F. Let stand for 15 to 20 minutes, or until the temperature rises to 145°F.

For medium, roast for 2 3/4 to 3 hours, or to an internal temperature of 145° to 150°F, depending on how much pink meat you like. Let stand for 15 to 20 minutes, or until the temperature rises to 160°F.

Carve and serve.

Makes 8 to 10 servings.

Fresh Salad Greens with Chive-Cream Dressing

MIX AN ASSORTMENT of fresh greens that a cook in early autumn St. Louis might have picked from her kitchen garden.

6 cups torn lettuce

1/2 cup sour cream

I tablespoon white wine vinegar

I teaspoon snipped chives

I teaspoon sugar

1/2 teaspoon salt

Dash of freshly ground black pepper

Rinse the lettuce and pat dry. Set aside. Stir together all the remaining ingredients and serve with lettuce.

Makes about 6 servings.

143

Spicy Sweet and Sour Pickles

THE NEWER AMERICANS imported their fermentation skills from Europe and made wines, vinegar, and, of course, whiskey. Vinegar, sugar, and salt preserve vegetables and fruits through the cold season.

2 pounds small cucumbers, unpeeled and cut into 3/8-inch slices

2 medium sweet spring onions, peeled and sliced vertically

1 1/2 cups white vinegar

1 1/2 cups sugar

2 tablespoons salt

2 teaspoons whole cloves

1 teaspoon whole celery seed

1 teaspoon mustard seed

1 teaspoon ground turmeric

1/2 teaspoon ground ginger

Layer slices of cucumbers and onions in a large glass bowl. Set aside.

Combine the vinegar, sugar, salt, cloves, celery seed, mustard seed, turmeric, and ginger. Stir gently until the sugar dissolves. Pour evenly over the cucumber-onion mixture. Toss gently. Place in the refrigerator, covered, for 5 days, stirring twice a day. Will keep in the refrigerator for up to 2 months (if you don't eat them first).

Makes 7 cups pickles.

Wild Grape Jelly

PEOPLE PICKED WILD grapes in the late summer and early fall for preserves and for homemade wine. The grape varieties *Vitis rupestris* or *Vitis aestiva* were common to the St. Louis area in 1806.

2 pounds wild or domestic grapes	2 cups sugar

Mash the grapes in a large saucepan. Bring to a rolling boil and boil for 15 minutes. Strain the juice through cheesecloth or a dishcloth. You will have about 1 1/2 cups of juice. Combine the juice and sugar. Bring to a rolling boil and boil for 20 minutes. Skim any residue from the top of the jelly. Pour into 3 clean 8-ounce jelly jars. Jelly will remain slightly soft.

Cover and store in the refrigerator or freezer.

Makes 3 cups jelly.

Nutmeg-Plum Shortcake

THE ST. LOUIS hosts and hostesses had their pick of summer fruits. Taste the contrast between this rich shortcake and the more rustic Prairie Plum Tart (see page 71).

PLUM SAUCE

2 pounds ripe plums

1/2 cup (firmly packed) brown sugar

1 teaspoon ground nutmeg

1 tablespoon cornstarch

SHORTCAKE

2 cups all-purpose flour

1/2 cup stone-ground cornmeal

1/4 cup sugar

1 tablespoon baking powder

1/2 teaspoon salt

1/2 cup butter

3/4 cup milk

1 egg

1 1/2 cups whipping cream, whipped

Slice the plums and remove the pits. Toss with the sugar and nutmeg and bring to a boil. Lower heat and cook about 20 minutes. In a small bowl, mix the cornstarch and 1/4 cup of water. Remove 1/2 cup of the hot sauce and stir into the cornstarch mixture. Add all at once to the plum sauce. Return to a boil and cook, stirring constantly, for about 1 minute, or until thickened. Set aside.

Mix the flour, cornmeal, sugar, baking powder, and salt. With 2 knives or a pastry blender, cut in the butter until the mixture is the size of shelled peas. Stir in the milk and egg and mix just until moistened. Spread in a well-greased 8-inch round baking dish. Bake in a 400° F oven for about 20 minutes, or until the top is golden brown.

Loosen the edges and carefully invert the pan. Slice the shortcake in half horizontally. Place the bottom on a serving plate. Top with half of the plum sauce. Add dollops of the whipped cream. Replace the top shortcake layer and top with the remaining cream. Drizzle the remaining plums over the cream and serve.

Makes about 8 servings.

Cream and Bread Pudding with Cherries

WHILE BREAD PUDDING is a traditional and practical way to use day-old bread, it becomes a more elegant dessert with dried cherries and cream.

1 cup dried cherries or raisins	4 eggs
2 tablespoons brandy	1/2 cup sugar
1/2 pound French bread, cut into 1/2-inch cubes (4 cups)	1 teaspoon grated lemon zest
2 1/2 cups warm half-and-half	1/2 teaspoon salt
2 cups milk	1/2 teaspoon ground nutmeg

147

Soak the cherries in brandy for 15 to 20 minutes. Remove the cherries from the brandy; reserve the brandy to add later. Layer the cherries and bread in a well-buttered 1 1/2 quart casserole. Heat 2 cups of the half-and-half and the 2 cups milk to just below boiling, or until small bubbles form around the edge and skin forms on top. Pour over the bread and cherries and let stand for about 30 minutes.

Beat together the eggs, sugar, brandy, lemon zest, salt, and nutmeg. Pour evenly over the bread and milk mixture. Bake in a 325°F oven. After 30 minutes, pour the remaining 1/2 cup half-and-half over the mixture. Bake 1 hour more, or until the mixture is set and a knife inserted in the middle comes out clean.

Makes 6 to 8 servings.

Almond Sponge Cake

FRONTIER ST. LOUIS received regular shipments of all kinds of goods, including almonds from Philadelphia via the Ohio River. Robert Fulton's successful steamboat operation, begun in 1807, eased two-way traffic and trade both down the Mississippi to New Orleans and up the Missouri as far as Fort Benton in what is now Montana.

4 eggs, separated, plus 1 whole egg

2 cups sugar

1/4 cup almond paste

2 cups all-purpose flour

2 teaspoons baking powder

1/2 teaspoon salt

1/4 cup milk

Lemon Curd (recipe follows), for serving

Beat the egg whites until stiff peaks form. Set aside. Combine the yolks, whole egg, sugar, and almond paste and beat well. Combine the flour, baking powder, and salt and add to the egg mixture alternately with the milk. Gently fold the eggs whites into the batter.

Grease only the bottom of a 10-inch tube pan. Pour the batter into the pan. Bake in a 350°F oven for about 40 minutes, or until the top is golden and a wooden pick inserted into the cake comes out clean. Cool right side up on a wire rack. Remove the cake to a serving plate. Serve with Lemon Curd.

Makes 8 servings.

Lemon Curd

2 cups sugar

Juice and grated zest
of 3 medium lemons
(about 1/2 cup juice)

1/2 cup butter

1/2 teaspoon salt

4 eggs, well beaten

Almond Sponge Cake
(see page 148), angel food cake,
or pound cake, for serving

Combine the sugar, lemon juice, zest, butter, and salt in a saucepan over medium-low heat. When the butter has melted, stir 1/4 cup of the hot liquid into the eggs. Add the eggs all at once to the sugar mixture, stirring constantly until thick, about 15 minutes. Serve with Almond Sponge Cake.

Makes 1 1/2 cups.

149

i Donald Jackson, ed., *Letters of the Lewis and Clark with Related Documents 1783 – 1854*, 2 volumes, (Urbana, Illinois: University of Illinois Press, 1978). Clark, 1:315.

ii Meriwether Lewis and William Clark, *The Journals of the Lewis and Clark Expedition*, 13 volumes, ed. Gary E. Moulton (Lincoln, Nebraska: University of Nebraska Press, 1983 – 2001). Clark, 8:315.

iii Ibid., 8:365.

iv Ibid., 8:359.

v Ibid., 8:363.

vi Ibid., 8:370-71.

vii *Thomas Jefferson Papers*, Manuscript Division, Library of Congress.

viii *Journals*, Ibid., Clark, 8:367.

-150-

Epilogue

COOKBOOKS RARELY HAVE conclusions, perhaps because a cookbook author accepts that a recipe is a fluid thing, subject to the whims and mood of the cook. History books, though, require a summation. The historian strives to neatly package the facts into their place in the long march of time—even though history is as resistant to one interpretation as recipes are to a single version.

We know the rest of the Lewis and Clark story. The Expedition forms an important piece of Thomas Jefferson's Presidential legacy. Meriwether Lewis adjusted poorly to a more settled life. He served as Governor of Louisiana territory and put off the task of writing a complete report of the journey. He died by his own hand on 11 October 1809 in Tennessee, en route from St. Louis to Washington, D.C.

Clark moved to St. Louis with his first wife, was twice widowed, and saw three of his seven children grow to adulthood, including the eldest who was named Meriwether Lewis Clark at his birth in January 1809. William Clark served as the chief Indian Agent and as Governor of Missouri Territory during his active, full life. He died 1 September 1838 in St. Louis.

Sacagawea sent her son Jean Baptiste to study in St. Louis under the wing of the Clark family. She is believed to have died in 1812 in what is now South Dakota.

In ever larger numbers, people moved to the United States and its territories on the promise of a better life than the one left in their native lands. They filled in the map, bringing Jefferson's vision to life. In another hundred years the journals' descriptions of immense buffalo herds and hundreds of fish caught in a single outing became the stuff of legend. The way of life that sustained the tribes for hundreds of years became fragile, often breaking under the onslaught of the newcomers.

Travelers in the early 1800s experienced a natural world that many long for in our technology- and information-packed age. The Expedition's bicentennial gives us the chance to glimpse the time before such innovations as the steam engine, the cookstove that replaced the open hearth, and the canning processes that helped shift how we think about where our food comes from and how we cook and eat it.

A globe's worth of food traditions have spread across North America since Lewis and Clark returned to their joyful 1806 homecoming in St. Louis. What we learn about the Expedition will nourish our understanding of the cultures nudging one another and blending in the twenty-first century.

151

---

[1] *Thomas Jefferson Papers*, Manuscript Division, Library of Congress.

Bibliography and Further Reading

Basin-Plateau Aboriginal Groups.
"Anthropological Papers."
American Ethnology Bulletin 119:17-31;
186-217. Washington, D.C.: Bureau
of American Ethnology, Smithsonian
Institution, 1938.

Beard, James. *James Beard's American Cookery.*
Boston: Little, Brown, 1972.

———. *The New James Beard.* New York:
Alfred A. Knopf, 1981.

Bronz, Ruth Adams. *Miss Ruby's
American Cooking.* New York:
Harper & Row, 1989.

Burroughs, Raymond Darwin, ed.
*The Natural History of the Lewis and
Clark Expedition.* East Lansing:
Michigan State University Press, 1995.

Carson, Jane. *Colonial Virginia Cookery.*
Williamsburg, Va.: Colonial
Williamsburg, 1968.

Child, Julia, Louisette Bertholle,
and Simone Beck. *Mastering the Art
of French Cooking.* New York:
Alfred A. Knopf, 1967.

Clark, William. *Dear Brother: Letters of William
Clark to Jonathan Clark.* Edited by James J.
Holmberg. New Haven: Yale University
Press, 2002.

Cutright, Paul Russell. *Lewis and Clark:
Pioneering Naturalists.* Lincoln:
University of Nebraska Press, 1969.

DeVoto, Bernard, ed. *The Journals of Lewis
and Clark.* Boston: Houghton Mifflin,
The American Heritage Library, 1953.

Engel, Allison and Margaret Engel.
Food Finds. New York: HarperCollins,
2000.

Fussell, Betty. *Crazy for Corn.* New York:
HarperCollins, Perennial, 1995.

———. *I Hear America Cooking.* New York:
Penguin Books, 1997.

Gilmore, Melvin R. *Uses of Plants by the Indians
of the Missouri River Region.* Lincoln:
University of Nebraska Press, 1977.

Goetzmann, William H., and Glyndwr
Williams. *The Atlas of North American
Exploration: From the Norse Voyages to the Race
to the Pole.* Norman: University of
Oklahoma Press, 1992.

Golden Schroeder, Lisa. *At Home with Bread.*
Minnetonka, Minn.: Cooking Club
of America, 2002.

Hanson, Charles E., Jr. "Sheet Iron
Kettles." *Museum of the Fur Trade Quarterly*
28 (1992 Spring): 2-6.

Heiser, Charles B., Jr. *Seed to Civilization.*
Cambridge: Harvard University Press,
1990.

Hines, Mary Anne, Gordon Marshall,
and William Woys Weaver. *The Larder
Invaded Reflection on Three Centuries of
Philadelphia Food and Drink.* Philadelphia:
Library Company of Philadelphia, 1986.

Holder, Preston. *The Hoe & the Horse on the
Plains.* Lincoln: University of Nebraska
Press, 1970.

Howe, Carrol B. *Ancient Tribes of the Klamath Country*. Portland, Oregon: Binford & Mort, 1968.

Hunn, Eugene S., with James Selam and Family. *Nch'i-Wána, "The Big River": Mid-Columbia Indians and Their Land*. Seattle: University of Washington Press, 1990.

Hunt, Robert R. "Gills and Drams of Consolation," *We Proceeded On* 17(3):19-27. 1991.

———. "Gills and Drams of Consolation," *We Proceeded On* 17(4):11-15. 1991.

Jackson, Donald, ed. *Letters of the Lewis and Clark Expedition with Related Documents: 1783-1854*. Urbana: University of Illinois Press, 1978.

Jefferson, Thomas. *Thomas Jefferson's Garden Book*. Edited by Edwin M Betts. Philadelphia: American Philosophical Society, 1999.

Jones, Evan. *American Food: The Gastronomic Story*. New York: Dutton, 1975.

Kavasch, Barrie. *Native Harvest: Recipes and Botanicals of the American Indian*. New York: Random House, Vintage Books, 1979.

Kindscher, Kelly. *Edible Wild Plants of the Prairie*. Lawrence: University Press of Kansas, 1987.

Leslie, Eliza. *Miss Leslie's Directions for Cookery*. Mineola, New York: Dover Publications, 1999.

———. *Seventy-Five Receipts for Pastry, Cakes, and Sweetmeats*. Bedford, Mass.: Applewood Books, 1993.

Lewis, Edna, and Mary Goodbody. *In Pursuit of Flavor*. Charlottesville: University Press of Virginia, 1988.

Lewis, Meriwether, and William Clark. *The Journals of the Lewis and Clark Expedition*, 13 Volumes. Edited by Gary E. Moulton. Lincoln: University of Nebraska, 1983-2001.

Loge, Anna. "We Encamped By Some Butifull Springs:" An Interpretation of Captain William Clark's Campsite on July 7, 1806. *We Proceeded On* 24(4):16-26. 1998.

Matthews, Daniel. *Cascade-Olympic Natural History*. Portland, Oregon: Raven Editions in conjunction with the Audubon Society of Portland, 1990.

Moerman, Daniel E. *Native American Ethnobotany*. Portland, Oregon: Timber Press, 1998.

Nichols, Nell B., ed., and Kathryn Larson. *Farm Journal's Country Cookbook*. Garden City, New York: Doubleday, 1959.

———. *Farm Journal's Freezing & Canning Cookbook*. Garden City, New York: Doubleday, 1973.

Randolph, Mary, with Historical Notes and Commentaries by Karen Hess. *The Virginia House-Wife*. Columbia: University of South Carolina Press, 1984.

Ronda, James P. *Lewis and Clark Among the Indians*. Lincoln: University of Nebraska Press, 1984.

Schlick, Mary Dodds. *Columbia River Basketry: Gift of the Ancestors, Gift of the Earth*. Seattle: University of Washington Press, 1994.

Scrimsher, Leda Scott. *Native Foods Used by the Nez Percé Indians of Idaho*. Unpublished dissertation. Moscow: University of Idaho, 1967.

Simmons, Amelia. *The First American Cookbook: A Facsimile of "American Cookery" 1796*. New York: Dover Publications, 1958.

Stein, Susan R. *The Worlds of Thomas Jefferson at Monticello*. New York: Abrams, in association with the Thomas Jefferson Memorial Foundation, Inc., 1993.

Tannahill, Reay. *Food in History*. New York: Stein and Day, 1973.

Weaver, William Woys. *Pennsylvania Dutch Country Cooking*. New York: Abbeville Press Publishers. 1993.

———. *35 Receipts from "The Larder Invaded."* Philadelphia: Library Company of Philadelphia, 1986.

Will, George F., and George E. Hyde. *Corn Among the Indians of the Upper Missouri*. Lincoln: University of Nebraska Press, 1964.

Bibliography, continued

Wilson, Gilbert. *Buffalo Bird Woman's Garden*. St. Paul: Minnesota Historical Society Press, 1987.

Ziemann, Hugo, and Mrs. F.L. Gillette. *The White House Cook Book*. New York: The Saalfield Publishing Company, 1920.

Zucker, Jay, and Kay Hummel. *Oregon Indians: Culture, History & Current Affairs, An Atlas & Introduction*. Portland: Press of the Oregon Historical Society, 1983.

154

Websites

Plant Identification and Description

NatureServe in partnership with the Nature Conservancy
www.natureserve.org

United States Department of Agriculture Plants Database
http://plants.usda.gov

Lewis and Clark

National Council Lewis and Clark Bicentennial
www.lewisandclark200.org

Lewis and Clark Trail Heritage Foundation
www.lewisandclark.org

Lewis and Clark on the Information Superhighway
www.lcarchive.org

Lewis and Clark National Historic Trail
www.nps.gov/lecl

Lewis and Clark Trail—Re-Live the Adventure of the Corps of Discovery
www.lewisandclarktrail.com

Monticello: Home of Thomas Jefferson
www.monticello.org

Food History

Food History News
www.foodhistorynews.com

Food Site of the Day
www.foodsiteoftheday.com

Gastronomica, The Journal of Food and Culture
www.gastronomica.org

History Cooks (Home of *The Food Journal of Lewis & Clark*)
www.historycooks.com

Mail-Order Sources

Meats*

Broken Arrow Ranch
Texas Wild Game Cooperative
P.O. Box 530
Ingram, Texas 78025
512.367.5875
Toll-free: 800.962.GAME (4263)
www.brokenarrowranch.com
Wild venison and wild antelope.

Broadbents B&B Food Products
6321 Hopkinsville Road
Cadiz, Kentucky 42211
Toll-free: 800.841.2202
www.broadbenthams.com
Country ham, country slab bacon, blackberry jam, beaten biscuits.

Triple U Buffalo Ranch
26314 Tatanka Road
Fort Pierre, South Dakota 57532
605.567.3624
Toll-free: 877.301.0796
www.tripleuranch.com
Third-generation buffalo ranch offering steaks, roasts, ground buffalo, and jerky.

North American Bison Cooperative
1658 Highway 281
P.O. Box 672
New Rockford, North Dakota 58356-0672
701.947.2505
Toll-free: 800.630.7363
www.buffalo-nickel.com
North Dakota-grown Buffalo-Nickel brand bison, including jerky and fresh products including roasts, steaks, and burger.

Sausage-Making Supplies

Road Runner Distributing Co.
4432 South 70th East Avenue
Tulsa, Oklahoma 74145
Toll-free: 800.331.2070
http://roadrunner-merit.com
Everything for sausage making, including casings, grinders, stuffers, and seasonings.

Smoked Fish*

Josephson's Smoked Fish
P.O. Box 412
Astoria, Oregon 97103
503.325.2190
Fax: 503.325.4075
Toll-free: 800.772.FISH (3474)
www.josephsons.com
Third-generation owned, offering cold-smoked salmon; hot-smoked salmon, sturgeon, trout, halibut, and shellfish; salmon jerky; and canned salmon and other seafood.

Karla's Krabs
Karla Steinhauser
P.O. Box 537
Rockaway Beach, Oregon 97136
503.355.2362
Fax: 503.355.9632
karlasfish@hotmail.com
Owner-produced for thirty-nine years. Smoked salmon, sturgeon, red trout, halibut, and oysters. Mail-order only; write or call for brochure.

*All meat and fish products processed under licensed inspection.

continued on next page

155

Mail-Order Sources, continued

Fruit Preserves

Eva Gates Homemade Preserves
P.O. Box 696
Bigfork, Montana 59911
406.837.4356
Toll-free: 800.682.4283
evagates@digisys.net
Third-generation owned, offering fruit preserves and syrups including wild huckleberry and chokecherry, black cap raspberry, and red raspberry.

The Huckleberry Patch
Highway 2
P.O. Box 1
Hungry Horse, Montana 59919
406.387.5000 or 6570
Toll-free: 800.527.7340
hucpatch@cyberport.net
Offering wild huckleberry and chokecherry, and black cap raspberry preserves, jelly, and syrups.

Homemade by Dorothy
5150 Montecito Place
Boise, Idaho 83704
208.375.3720
Toll-free: 800.657.7449
www.dorothys.cc
Second-generation owned, offering wild huckleberry and chokecherry, black raspberry, and blackberry preserves.

Garden Seeds

Seeds of Change
P.O. Box 15700
Santa Fe, New Mexico 87506
Toll-free: 888.762.7333
http://store.yahoo.com/seedsofchange
Heirloom and traditional seeds, including Mandan red flour corn and Lakota winter squash.

Seed Savers Exchange
3076 North Winn Road
Decorah, Iowa 52101
563.382.5990
www.seedsavers.org
Heirloom and traditional seeds.

Thomas Jefferson Center for Historic Plants Twinleaf Catalogue
P.O. Box 316
Charlottesville, Virginia 22902
www.twinleaf.org

Gift Baskets

Pierre Street Emporium
321 Pierre Street
Pierre, South Dakota 57501
605.776.0200
Toll-free: 888-807-1048
www.dakotashop.com/SOUTH DAKOTAgifts
Buffalo jerky, popcorn, and wild fruit preserves, including chokecherry, Juneberry, buffalo berry, plum, grape.

Whole Grains and Beans

Bob's Red Mill
5209 Southeast International Way
Milwaukie, OR 97222
Toll-free: 800.349.2173
www.bobsredmill.com
Source for stone-ground corn meal, whole wheat flour, hazelnuts, and an extensive assortment of other grains, beans, and baking supplies.

For more mail-order food resources across the United States, consult Food Finds by Allison Engel and Margaret Engel.

156

Recipe Index

159

Historical Index

162

medical skills of, 124; partnership with Lewis,
32. *See also* specific topics

Clatsop Indians, 112, 115

Coboway, Chief, 124

Coffee, 53; Clark's comment about, 91

Collins, John, 42

Colter, John, 137

Columbia River, 30, 100, 102, 112, 120, 124;
ducks of, 121: maps, 113, 125; mussel shells
of, 61; salmon of, 128

Cooking, in baskets, 111; camas root, 109;
Charbonneau's, 96; Hidatsa, 93; notes from
Clark, 111; Shoshone, 93; snow for, 108;
St. Louis, 38; tribal, 82; by York, 58

Coot, 121

Corn, Arikara, seeds from, 5; Buffalo Bird
woman and, 78, 84; at Camp DuBois, 44,
46; blacksmithing skills in exchange for, 82,
83; bread made from with beans, 73; dent,
45, dried/drying, 73, 83; eaten with
Shoshone, 107; gift of, 72, 136; green or
sweet corn, 82, 138; grown by settlers, 32,
35; gummy, 84; hulling, 88; Huron, among,
39; Mandans, seeds from 5, 136, 137; mill,
16, 82; Narragansett, among, 39; provisions,
54, 56; reserved for later, 100; seeds, 5;
traded for, 72, 73, 76, 82, 83, 84, 137, 139.
See also Corn Meal, Hominy

Cornmeal, 110; at Camp DuBois, 44;
Detachment orders, 54; in hoe cakes, 43;
provisions, 53; in puddings, 22, 46; in
scrapple, 22

Corps of Discovery, 2. *See also,* Expedition,
Food, Hunting, Trading

Cous, 128, 132; described, 114, 127; eaten with
bear oil, 129; edible vs. poisonous varieties, 129

Crops, 35, Buffalo Bird Woman's descriptions
of, 78; Jefferson's request for information
concerning, 30. *See also* Food, Gardens

Cruzatte, Pierre, 63, 130, 134

Cutler, Reverend Manasseh, 5

D-E

Dalles, 128

Deer, hunting for, 47, 62, 69, 80, 108,
131, 139; and Seaman, 33; taste of, 69.
See also Venison

Delaware Indians, 32

Detachment orders by Lewis, 42, 54, 56

Dickerson, Mahlon, 15

Dog, Lewis and Clark comment on as food, 114

Drouillard, George, 119

Duck, 47, 122; canvasback, 121

Edge, John, 56

Eggs, 44, 46, 122

Elk, 124; as food, 62, 68, 70, 118; hunting, 62,
63, 69, 80, 94, 113, 119, 134, 139

England/English, food traditions, 24, 142;
trade with, 15

Expedition, authorized, 12; bicentennial, 151;
instructions from Jefferson for, 30; legacy of,
137, 150; return of, 140, 150; seeds and
cuttings from, 5. *See also* Corps of Discovery,
Foods, Hunting, Trading

F

Farming/farms, 48. *See also* Gardens

Fat, animal, 47, 95, 96. *See also* specific type,
i.e., Lard

Fennel, 114, 126, 127

Fermentation, 144

Fields, Joseph, 66, 118

Fish, 2, 61, 94, 110, 128, 150; pounded, 112,
115, 118; supplies for catching, 16. *See also*
Catfish, Salmon, Whale

Flour, 2, 34, 51; as provision, 51, 53, 54, 104,
137; reserved, 100, 117

Floyd, Charles, 64

Food, 2; preservation of, 8, 36, 68, 78, 82, 83,
144, 152; rations, 52; traditions, 78, 151.
See also locations, Provisions, Recipes, specific
foods, specific tribes

Fort Clatsop, 2, 118, 121; about, 112; holidays
at, 118; departure from, 124; map of, 113;
trade at, 82, 83

Fort Mandan, 81, 82; about, 76; departure
from, 90, 91; map of, 77

France/French, 15; food, 40, 96; founding of
St. Louis, 40; presence, 77; sale of Louisiana
territory by, 12; translators of, 106

Fricassée, derivation of word, 20

Fruits, 62, 71, 139, 144, 146; orchard, 36;
preservation of, 144; wild, 36. *See also* Berries,
Plums, Lemons, Apples

G

Gallatin, Albert, 100; river named for, 100

Game. *See* Hunting, Meat

Gardening/gardens, 77; Jefferson's, 4, 9;
in northern plains, 114. *See also* Arikara,
Hidatsa, and Mandan

Garden Kalendar, 4

Gass, Patrick, 64

German food, 15, 24

Geese, 108

Gibson, Charles, 118

Goodbird, Edward, 78

Goodfellow, Elizabeth Coane, 23, 28
Grapes, wild, 62, 67, 145
Great Falls of Missouri River, 97, 133
Great Plains, berries in, 87; buffalo in, 106;
    fruits in, 87; hunting in, 80; map of Winter
    camp, 77; pemmican, 81; trading centers, 77,
    78; vegetables in, 85; winter camp, 88
Greens, 58, 143
Grizzly bear, 125
Groundnut, 37
Gummy corn, 84

H

Hazelnut, 110
Hall, Hugh, 42
Hardtack, 24, 70; trading for, 137
Harpers Ferry, 14, 97
Hinds, Bev, 130
Hidatsa Indians, 2, 76, 81, 87, 93, 102, 136;
    advised by, 90; gardens of, 72, 73, 77;
    translated by, 90, 106. *See also* Buffalo Bird
    Woman, Sacagawea
Hoe cakes, 56
Holding Eagle, Louise, 81, 84
Hominy, 44; about, 45; how to make, 45, 79;
    Mandan dish, 79; in provisions, 53, 57, 73
Honey, and bees, 34
Horses, 30, 32, 67; as food, 108; Nez Percé,
    108, 124; Shoshone, 102, 103
Hudson, Marilyn, 81, 84
Hunters/hunting, 2, 47, 48, 103; buffalo, 66,
    69, 108; Drouillard, 119; Fields, 66, 69; in
    Great Plains, 80, 81; Lewis shot while, 134;
    in middle Missouri, 139; in mountains, 129;
    in Northwest, 102, 107, 108, 109, 112; in
    Ohio River Valley, 30. *See also* specific animals
Huron Indians, 39

I-J-K

Ice cream, in Philadelphia, 15, 26
Illinois, Wood River, 32. *See also* Camp DuBois
Jean Baptiste, 2, 136; born, 87, education, 150
Jefferson, Thomas, correspondence with Lewis,
    4, 14, 30, 150; culinary interests, 2, 4, 5, 7,
    10; as envoy to France, 12; gardens of, 4, 9;
    instructions for Expedition, 30, 52; legacy of,
    150; recipes recorded by, 5, 7, 10; as
    Secretary of State, 12; Virginia roots of, 5;
    vision of, 4, 12, 14, 30, 150
Jefferson River, 102; named, 100
Jerky, 70; history of, 68; pemmican in, 81
Jerusalem artichoke, 92, 107
Keelboat, 32, 47, 52, 88

Kentucky, Louisville, 32
Kilamox Indian village, whale washed ashore at,
    113

L

LaBiche, François, 106
La Charette, 140
Lard, 81; for pie crust, 40; provisions, 32, 53,
    54, 79
Lemhi Valley, 102, 103, 106
Lemons, 26; invention of lemon custard, 28
Leslie, Eliza, 23
Lewis, Edna, 57
Lewis, Meriwether, background of, 5; birthday,
    63; correspondence, 4, 14, 30, 33, 140, 150;
    detachment orders, 42, 54, 56; and iron-
    frame boat, 97; letter to mother, 30; life after
    Expedition, 150; partnership with William
    Clark, 32; in Philadelphia, 15; preparation for
    Expedition, 12, 14, 19; shot by mistake, 134.
    See also specific topics
Lolo Hot Springs, 133
Lotus, 37
Louisiana Purchase, 12, 32, 40
Louisville, Kentucky, 32

M

Mackenzie, Alexander, 12
Madison, James, 100, river named for
Mandan Indians, 2, 76, 81, 136, 137;
    food/gardens, 5, 72, 73, 77, 107, 138;
    Sheheke-shote, 76, 136, 138; trade with, 82,
    83, 84
Maple sugar, 42
Maps: Bitterroots to the Pacific, 103; Columbia
    to Confluence of Missouri and Yellowstone,
    125; Great Plains Winter Camp, 77; Lower
    Missouri, 52, Middle Missouri, 67; St. Louis,
    137; Pacific Coast Winter Camp and
    Columbia Estuary, 113; Philadelphia to Camp
    DuBois, 33; Philadelphia, 15; United States,
    viii-1; Upper Missouri, 91; Washington, 5
Marias River, 133
Marks, Lucy, Lewis's mother, 30
Mayan Indians, 45
Meat, 2, 32, 50, 68, 109, 112, 134; amounts,
    47, 66, 67, 91, 99, 131; at Great Falls, 97;
    Lewis's craving for, 117; in mountains, 129;
    in Northwest, 109; near St. Louis, 139.
    See also specific animal
Milk, at Camp DuBois, 44
Mincemeat, history of, 8
Minnesota Historical Society, 78

Missouri River, 2, 32, 37, 42, 61, 66, 87, 136, 148, 150; cache left on, 118; current of, 47; frozen, 88; Great Falls of, 97, 133; headwaters of, 102; Jefferson talks about, 30, 150; maps including, 52, 67, 91, 125, 137; Three Forks of, 100, 102, 133; and Yellowstone River, 133

Missouri salsify, 5

Monticello, 4; gardens at, 9

Morel mushrooms, 130

Mountains, Bitterroots, 2, 97; 1805 crossing, 90, 100, 108, 109; 1806 crossing, 129; Rocky, 12, 40

Mussels, 61

N-O

Napoleon, and Louisiana Purchase, 12

Narragansett Indians, 39

Natchez Trace, 40

Native tribes, 2, 3, 32 124, 150; food of, 36, 39, 46, 56, 82, 127; gardening skills of, 114; relations with, 32, 66, 76, 124; trade with, 14, 53, 82, 83, 115. *See also* Food, specific food, specific tribal name

New Year's Day, at Camp DuBois, 50; at Fort Clatsop, 118

Nez Percé, 2; dependence upon, 124, 129; food/cooking of, 109, 120, 125, 127

Northwest, baskets in, 111; berries in, 104, 112, 121; food, 37, 106, 114, 128; hunting in, 102, 107, 108, 109, 112; map of, 103; rain in, 112; roots in, 37, 109, 114. *See also* specific food, tribal name

Ohio River, 33, 40, 148; departure on, 32; food in region of, 33; map of, 33; trade on, 40, 148

Onions, 126, 127, 137

Opossums, as food, 47

Ordway, Sgt. John, 2, 54, 64, 86, 98; about food and spirits, 74, 84, 86, 98

P

Pacific Northwest. *See* Northwest

Pawpaws, 139

Peabody Museum, basket in, 111

Pearl ash, 44

Peas, English, 9

Pemmican, 68, 81, 114

Pennsylvania Dutch, 23

Pepperpot, history of, 21

Philadelphia, 2, 14, 15; cuisine/food, 21, 23, 24, 26, 27; Lewis in, 15; map of, 15; Provisions, 16–17; and trade, 15, 38, 40, 148

Pigeons, as food, 132

Pine nuts, 127

Pirogues (perogues), 47, 52, 88, 140; purchased, 32. *See also* Canoes

Pittsburgh, 30, 32

Plateau tribes, 111, 114

Plums, 71, 87, 139

Pork (pigs), food as, 32, 44; last of, 102; left in cache, 97; provisions as, 51, 53, 54; raised, 32; traded for, 137

Portable soup, food as, 108; history of, 19; how to make, 18; as provisions, 16

Potatoes, Clark compares to wapato, 115; described, 37; history of, 37

Potlatch, 112

Prairie turnip, called white apple, 93; common turnip as substitute for, 93; digging, 93; as food gathered by Sacagawea, 93; Lewis's opinion of, 94; mentioned, 37

President's House, 5

Provisions, 53, 54, 73; buying/securing, 14, 16, 17, 30, 51, 53, 54; detachment orders from Lewis for, 42, 54, 56; 73; from whale, 113

Pryor, Nathaniel, 64

Puddings, 46, 74

R

Rabbit, the animal, as food, 67; -berry, 74

Rain, at Fort Clatsop, 112

Rations, *See* Provisions

Rhode Island, corn in, 39

Rocky Mountains, 12, 40, 100

Roots, 2, 37, 47; camas, 109, 114, 129; cous, 114, 129; in Great Plains, 90, 92, 93, 94; in mountains, 129; in Northwest, 107, 109, 114, 115, 127; poison varieties, 129; trading, 114, 115. *See also* specific foods, specific tribes

S

Sacagawea (Sakakawea), 2, 87, 95, 97, 102, 116, 133; and Clark, 133, 136; demands to see whale, 113; and Hidatsa, 87; food gathering and preparation by, 90, 92, 93, 115, 116, 127; joins Expedition, 76, 87; life after Expedition, 150; as mother, 2, 87, 90, 150; return to home, 136; and Shoshone, 93, 103, 106; as translator, 90, 106; voting, 112

St. Charles, 35, 52

St. Louis, 52, 88, 124, 136, 139, 145, 146; about, 40; as Clark's home, 150; food traditions in, 40, 141; goods sold in, 38; home to, 140, 150

Salish Indians, 108

Salmon, 106, 111, 120, 128; blueback, 128;

Bite into the Adventure of a Lifetime!

YES, I WANT _____ copies *of The Food Journal of Lewis & Clark: Recipes for an Expedition*, at $19.95 each, plus $6 shipping (UPS Ground) for the first book and $2 for each additional book. (South Dakota residents please add $1.20 sales tax per book). Allow 15 days for delivery.

TO PLACE YOUR ORDER:

Call toll-free to order using your credit card: 877-581-8422
or fax this form with your credit card order: 605-668-9586
or use our secure ordering at www.HistoryCooks.com
mail to: History Cooks, P.O. Box 709, Yankton, SD 57078

☐ Please charge my: ☐ VISA   ☐ MC   ☐ AmEx   ☐ Discover

Credit Card Number _____

Signature _____ Exp. date _____/_____

☐ Please autograph my book (s) to _____

Name _____

Organization _____

Address (no P.O. Boxes, please) _____

_____

City _____ State _____ Zip _____

Email _____ Phone _____

☐ Please send information about History Cooks Paleocuisineology® presentations.

Thank You